THE
Light
STREAMED
BENEATH IT

SHAWN HITCHINS

A Memoir of Grief and Celebration

THE
Light
STREAMED

BENEATH IT

This book is also available as a Global Certified Accessible™ (GCA) ebook. ECW Press's ebooks are screen reader friendly and are built to meet the needs of those who are unable to read standard print due to blindness, low vision, dyslexia, or a physical disability.

Published by ECW Press
665 Gerrard Street East
Toronto, Ontario, Canada M4M 1Y2
416-694-3348 / info@ecwpress.com

Get the eBook free!*
*proof of purchase required

Purchase the print edition and receive the eBook free. For details, go to ecwpress.com/eBook.

Editor for the Press: Crissy Calhoun
Cover design: Michel Vrana

To the best of his abilities, the author has related experiences, places, people, and organizations from his memories of them. In order to protect the privacy of others, he has, in some instances, changed the names of certain people and details of events and places.

LIBRARY AND ARCHIVES CANADA CATALOGUING IN PUBLICATION

Title: The light streamed beneath it : a memoir of grief and celebration / Shawn Hitchins.

Names: Hitchins, Shawn, author.

Identifiers: Canadiana (print) 20210177748 | Canadiana (ebook) 20210177942

ISBN 978-1-77041-561-4 (softcover)
ISBN 978-1-77305-788-0 (ePub)
ISBN 978-1-77305-789-7 (PDF)
ISBN 978-1-77305-790-3 (Kindle)

Subjects: LCSH: Hitchins, Shawn. | LCSH: Entertainers—Canada—Biography. | CSH: Authors, Canadian (English)—21st century—Biography. | LCSH: Gay men—Canada—Biography. | LCSH: Bereavement. | LCGFT: Autobiographies.

Classification: LCC PN2308.H59 A3 2021 | DDC 792.702/8092—dc23

We acknowledge the support of the Canada Council for the Arts. *Nous remercions le Conseil des arts du Canada de son soutien.* This book is funded in part by the Government of Canada. *Ce livre est financé en partie par le gouvernement du Canada.* We acknowledge the support of the Ontario Arts Council (OAC), an agency of the Government of Ontario, which last year funded 1,965 individual artists and 1,152 organizations in 197 communities across Ontario for a total of $51.9 million. We also acknowledge the support of the Government of Ontario through the Ontario Book Publishing Tax Credit, and through Ontario Creates.

ONTARIO ARTS COUNCIL
CONSEIL DES ARTS DE L'ONTARIO
an Ontario government agency
un organisme du gouvernement de l'Ontario

Canada Council for the Arts
Conseil des arts du Canada

Canada

PRINTED AND BOUND IN CANADA

PRINTING: MARQUIS 5 4 3 2 1

MIX
Paper from responsible sources
FSC
www.fsc.org
FSC® C103567

This work is dedicated to the life, laughter, and love of
Matthew James Hines
muse, cheerleader, soulmate, cuspy Leo

And is in loving memory of
David Francisco Martinez
awakener, hurricane, lover, typical Sagittarius

"Let everything happen to you: beauty and terror.
Just keep going. No feeling is final."

— RAINER MARIA RILKE, *THE BOOK OF HOURS*

*"It's very difficult to keep the line between the past and the present . . .
Do you know what I mean? Awfully difficult."*

— LITTLE EDIE, *GREY GARDENS*

AUTHOR'S NOTE

My story and my loss intersect and collide with many others'. We do not know emotional landscapes outside our own; we can only hold space for contrasting viewpoints. My testimony exists as a whole and as part of a greater whole. I've taken care to refer to a few individuals by their archetypes, combine several individuals into one character, or respectfully omit them.

Part of my work in healing includes investigating traditions and rituals from cultures and religions outside of my ancestry. I enter these conversations with humility. I combine quiet study with firsthand practice. I listen to the wisdom of my teachers and the traditions of their ancestors. I hold these knowings with reverence, separate from myself, and do not confuse or represent them as my own.

BEGINNING

> *"Marley was dead: to begin with.*
> *There is no doubt whatever about that."*
>
> — CHARLES DICKENS, *A CHRISTMAS CAROL*

I am not Dickens, the master of both beginnings and endings. So I'll borrow an opening line from him. *Matthew and David were dead: to begin with.*

I sob every time I encounter *A Christmas Carol*, the tale of Ebenezer Scrooge and his holiday hauntings. I don't weep for Tiny Tim and his sacred catchphrase, "God bless Us, Every One!" I couldn't give a fig about Tiny Tim, but it's full waterworks when Scrooge wakes up a changed man just in time for Christmas morning. The miser is granted something more precious than gold: he is granted time. His fears and regrets turn to joy and elation, and he is transformed. He moves forward embodying the spirit of the past, present, and future in equal measure. A junior school production of this scene featuring a prepubescent

Scrooge wearing a cotton ball beard and a flannel dress would still make me bawl. This child could shout through a cardboard window, "What's to-day, my fine fellow?" to a twill-cap-wearing fetus who answers, shredding a cockney accent, "To-day! Why, CHRISTMAS DAY!" and my ducts simply would not withstand the pressure.

My feelings have feelings.

Dickens created a character who wakes up in his own experience after an overnight process of psychoanalysis decades before Jung or Freud were even subconscious. I could liken Scrooge's journey to a spiritual awakening, but his transformation is deeper, darker. He is chilled to his marrow in a direct confrontation with death. His return to aliveness is a journey through death, disease, humor, and trauma — all baked in a jolly Victorian suet pudding.

I have witnessed horror, felt haunted, undergone intense therapy, and now I am awake. I, like Scrooge, am gifted precious time.

Matthew and David are dead: to begin with.

I repeat this fact to myself daily, over and over to carve new grooves in my brain. To accept this fresh reality. They were living, then they were not living. They lived, they died, and now their nicknames are permanently inked on my body. *There is no doubt whatever about that.* Matt's exuberant "ELBY!" is etched in caps on my right wrist and David's elegant cursive "Shew" is carved onto my left ribs. Their handwriting was lifted from love letters and transferred in fine black ink by the same gobsmacked tattoo artist who offered that all pain is temporary.

It's important for me to tell you now that they are dead, at the very beginning. Their deaths are not plot twists in a misery memoir, nor teasers or shiny lures for morbid curiosity. Their deaths are their own. I am not Matt's accident, nor am I David's death by suicide. Defining what is and is not personal in the wake of loss is the difficult work of grief — especially when shame and anger enter the conversation.

What is personal are my individual relationships to these beautiful men and the thick connections that we formed. What is personal are the imprints left on me from coaching Matt to let go, from begging David to hold on. What is personal is being forced to wear an invisible dunce cap of grief that read "impossibly sad" for months and months and months. It is personal that I lost two great loves within five months of each other, and I emerged from this experience with an understanding that life is essentially good. It is certainly not fair — but it is good. This is the point. Life is good.

And so here we are. You and I, entering this intimate conversation. *Life is good.*

I reread *A Christmas Carol* on a bright and sunny September day, in a Toronto park with maple trees full of green leaves not yet crisped by the fall air. Winter was the furthest thing from my thoughts. I love the simplicity of how Dickens draws characters, how he used the ancient values and rituals of Saturnalia (the Roman celebration of Saturn/Dionysus) to redefine Christmas for the masses; I love how he upheld the very Victorian ideal that the future can be altered; I love how death was indivisible from the day-to-day experience of Victorians. It was the first book that kept my attention, outside the canon of death literature that had arrived at my doorstep — paired with casseroles. All those were essential reads, but not one included a road map back to the living like *A Christmas Carol.*

The time to learn about death is not just in the eye of a shitstorm of loss; death is also a conversation for still waters and blue skies. Death is an anytime conversation. Our fast-paced individualist lifestyles, weakened community ties, and rejection of theology have left us ill-prepared for the most significant event of our existence next to our births. We don't know how to incorporate death and dying into our day-to-day lives, to sit with our grief. Death has been ushered to the shadows. When tragedy strikes, we fall back on cultural norms and restrained mourning to streamline or bypass any pain. There is vital data in our discomfort and pain, information that can heal ourselves, heal communities.

This story is my path back to aliveness. This story is both an elegy of my body and a ballad for two dynamic men who changed my life — two men who suddenly vanished.

My glaciers are melting. Glaciers, that is what Matt and David were to me, formed layer by layer with edges both smooth and rough, dignified in length, width, and depth, and created (as it felt to me) by some greater design. They are melting away. It is evaporation, compression, and recession that reduces a slow-moving river of ice into a watery till of rocks, sand, and clay. Grief is collapse. It's the suspended details of a life that were once held and co-supported suddenly crashing to the earth; it is the rubble of evidence, the knickknacks, T-shirts, birthday cards, and photos. It's the loss of a language. It's the transformation of complicated individuals into saints stripped of sexuality. It's intimate stories without a corroborating witness, inside jokes without a playful collaborator. I feel an urgency to capture these loves before they disappear, to chart their vastness with the wonder of an astronomer, map their intricacies with the curiosity of an anthropologist, and capture their magic with the awe of a mystic.

As I type, I sit with my two toughest teachers. I wear their sweaters, I hold talismans they once held, and memorial candles are lit on a permanent altar next to my desk. I sense Matt stoically judging from the sidelines, and I hear David provoke me, "Shawn, can you just let it be messy?" My bereavement process was long and messy, but it wasn't all sadness and tears; it was weighted but not always heavy. There were long communal dinners, much laughter, sex, reflective hikes, dancing, moments of silence, witchcraft, yoga, carafes of coffee, and ever more casseroles.

Then there were the random acts of kindness. Like my neighbor Ed, who planted marigolds in the flower beds surrounding my apartment the summer following the tragedies. He felt a deep affection for Matt and was charmed instantly by David. One day, while passing in the lobby of the building, Ed randomly asked my favorite flower. I said marigolds, having learned that the vibrant petals help light the way for visiting spirits. At the end of July, hundreds of yellow and orange blooms lined a pathway right beneath my open third-floor windows.

"Marigolds also help keep the squirrels away." Ed winked.

As we fly in and out of scenes, like Scrooge and his spirit guides, visiting the "shadows of the things that have been," know that these words are the flesh, skin, and bones of my experience. In overwhelming moments, feel me reassure you that all is okay, as I whispered to Matt in his final moments. Feel my hand press against your collarbone soothing, calming as it calmed David as we drove across the Bay Bridge towards Oakland.

We begin our journey in San Francisco, a city currently undergoing a second Victorian age. An age where the life expectancy of a man was forty, one's value was in their productivity, income inequality was vast, and a writer got paid a penny per word.

Now, like Scrooge, who begged the Ghost of Christmas Yet to Come to "see some tenderness connected with a death," we walk with the black-cloaked figure who beckons us forward.

FLESH

February 9, 2018

I struggled in San Francisco to find any experience that would straddle its two extremes, anything to make it more tolerable and less inhumane. This was my disappointment after spending ten days exploring the city. California is a stunning embarrassment of riches, but to be in San Francisco was to tiptoe around human suffering. My first step off the BART escalator into the tourist core of Union Square was greeted by a homeless man projectile vomiting on the sidewalk. This city laid bare the realities of income inequality, invasive tech industry, and gentrification. Where the population is divided sharply between those who have a home and those who do not. Those with housing are seen, their homes stacked on hills like raked auditorium seats offering stunning views of the bay. Those without shelter are hidden in the basin and seen only by a tourist not numb to the sights of unwashed genitals, intravenous drug use, and sidewalks covered in human excrement.

I felt unsafe as I walked from my hotel on the edge of the Tenderloin to meet someone I'd charmed online through wordplay. Getting up this early in the morning for a "no-pressure coffee chat" was a personal first. Meeting at seven meant having to get up at five thirty to pack for a noon flight back to Toronto. The rendezvous point seemed suspect, but I was promised it was an authentic American diner. The idea of drinking coffee from a cup and saucer, the clanking of the teaspoons, and empty creamers piled like top hats was enough to make sure I didn't sleep through my alarm.

I entered Sears Fine Food and walked through the checkered tiled foyer lined with antique Hoosier cabinets, towards a golden slot machine with a turkey dinner grand prize. I felt tentative, second-guessing this meeting while preparing for disappointment. I turned left at the one-armed bandit and saw a gorgeous man sitting at the lunch counter. He wore a blue Levi's denim jacket, he was tall, his hair was dark with a wave of curl, and his beard was full. He smiled while reading the *New York Times*.

"David?" I croaked — my first spoken word of the day.

David looked at me and my heart stopped. *You're out of your league.* He matched his profile. *A modern-day unicorn.*

"Hey Shawn." He had a generous smile.

David and I had started messaging as soon as I landed in the Bay Area. As I explored his city, I offered him blunt feedback on his freshly activated Scruff profile. Back and forth, I nixed his photos and suggested copy edits until I wrote, "It's perfect (for me). Finally. We can meet," sent with a winking emoji. He agreed. The flirtation between us was refreshing, a change from the more scripted interactions, the monosyllabic conversations geared towards getting off (and needing someone's quick help to achieve it). I was struggling following the end of a six-year common-law partnership. My breakup devastated me. Plus, in the years I was joyously attached, dating and hookup culture had migrated to apps. I entered the digital game a single *Homo erectus* trying to spark a connection with an iPhone. I found the sexually charged grid, without stranger danger or boundaries, flat and reductive. But the apps provided access to a community as I traveled solo and buried any real relationship potential with ceaseless work. Scrolling and flicking through profiles made being alone, exhausted, and away from my own bed somewhat tolerable. Months of ghosting and being ghosted by penises, torsos, and Ray-Ban sunglasses made David's authentic smile all the more magnetizing.

David gestured to the place setting beside him. I sat down on the red vinyl and chrome bar stool and swiveled my body towards him. A waitress moved from one end of the bar, filled my cup with piping hot coffee, and moved back without breaking her conversation with a regular. David passed me a milk creamer and we began to talk. I slid my saucer and cup towards him so I could rest my elbow on the countertop and prop myself up in an attempt not to slouch.

What I found most engaging about David was how he steered away from the dating script, the standard questions that gay men (of a certain age) ask each other when they first meet — the quiz portion that turns any date into a psych evaluation. He didn't ask me about my coming out story, how integrated my family was in my adult life, or whether I had explored sex with women before declaring my sexuality. In return, I didn't ask him his thoughts on the party scene, marriage, or children. These seemingly banal talking points are folded into the culture to quickly gauge trauma, stability, addiction, class, monogamy. Instead, we did a deep dive, found a natural rhythm, and landed on topics that made it feel like we were old souls who could make each other laugh. His laugh was generous, warm; his voice, resonant. He had an adorable small tremor in his right hand.

He vibrates with life.

Still, we padded our career achievements into our back and forth. David was a former dancer for the Martha Graham Company in New York. He had toured the world and bounced from coast to coast before ultimately calling the Bay Area his home. He found a second career in marketing and worked for the tech giants, but was currently studying embodiment at the Strozzi Institute to become a somatic coach. He was building a methodology for nervous system regulation. Everything he said was compelling, and I made a mental note to Google what the fuck the words somatic, embodiment, methodology, and Strozzi meant. I made sure to tell him that I was touring film festivals, doing national press interviews for my book, and had flown to LA for the first time to meet with a studio. My bizarre career had always been a shiny object to dangle in front of strangers, but it seemed matter of fact for David. As if one should be successful with many lives and ridiculous stories.

There were markers in his life that paralleled my own, and it was easy to find commonalities and trade our experiences. We both loved the performance artists Taylor Mac and Justin Vivian Bond, and one-upped each other on our proximity to them. We were both fresh(-ish) from relationships. I stood outside myself asking, "Am I having coffee and being absolutely charming with my gorgeous future husband?" *A move to California is a natural career step.* David was on his third mug of coffee and I had barely touched my first when he broke his attention from me to tune into his device. We both were conscious of his nine o'clock meeting, and I still had to check out of my hotel. He shifted on his stool in preparation to taper off our conversation. Vacation Mode took over me.

"Do you like cashews?" I blurted.

"I do. Why do you ask?"

"'Cause I have a whole bag at my hotel that I need to get rid of before I fly. Maybe you should come back to my room and eat some."

"You only want to eat cashews?" He tested my bravado.

"Well . . ."

David squiggled a checkmark towards our waitress. Between dropping plates of bacon and eggs, our exhausted server walked the length of the diner bar with our bill and a token for the slot machine. I pulled ten dollars out of my wallet for the five-and-change owing, while David began a hard negotiation session with the waitress for an extra token. She was impervious to David's tactics, a rock in upholding the house rule of one token per bill until David smiled and she softened long enough to reach into her apron and pull out a second chance at winning.

"Good luck with this one." She tossed the slug on the black countertop.

"Thanks!" I grinned.

He is a charmer.

We made our way towards the slot machine. David guided me by pressing his hand against my lower back, a first touch that rippled through my body and challenged my balance. David inserted his coin first into the machine. He pulled the lever and the three drums of the gold machine spun and slowly stopped and David dimmed in disappointment. Seconds later his hand returned to my lower back, and it was my turn to test fate.

"What if I win? Three thousand miles is a long way to travel for a free turkey dinner."

"Put the damn coin in, and let's go eat some cashews." David smirked.

Moments later we poured turkeyless out of Sears Fine Food. An uphill slope prevented us from breaking into a run as we sped up Powell Street, onto Sutter, into the hotel lobby. As we shared a cramped elevator with housekeeping and swaggered down the hallway to my room, David's hand remained pressed against my back, a junction for the energy that flowed between us.

The walls of room 708 were a garish avocado green with canary crown moldings and floral accents. It somehow worked. I am particular about hotels. I can't sleep in a room with two queen beds. I retire all the informational tent cards and guest room directories to a drawer. I put on the TV before I leave the suite. Something is unnerving about coming back to a quiet empty hotel room laden with instructional collateral on every surface. The only thing I enjoy about a hotel is not having to make my bed.

David spun me in tight. We kissed. The curves of our lips, chin, and nose fit perfectly. My hands slid between our bodies and I husked off his coat, peeling it inside-out over his shoulders and onto the floor. David's hands searched underneath my layers of jersey knit and up my torso so that one palm rested on my chest and the other down the back of my underwear. Our pelvises ground together.

"What about the cashews?" David whispered.

"Fuck the cashews!" I proclaimed before tipping our bodies onto the unmade bed.

We paused to deal with the practicality of protruding wallets, noisy pocket change, and valuable iPhones. We spoke a common language as we tested the depth and pressure of our lips with kisses that moved from gentle to vigorous. Our palms surveyed the new landscapes, thumbs kneading into tight muscles, fingers like paint-brushes caressed the skin until they found a way to squeeze each other's hardness. We broke out in smiles. David sat up and began to strip for me. His body was broad, his arms were muscular, and his legs were sculpted. There was a natural softening that made him human; his demigod status as a dancer had long been retired. I reciprocated by pulling off my clothes and throwing them across the room.

He held my gaze.

Naked, I felt the need to distract from my more-than-human body.

"What a lucky birthmark." I pointed to his right thigh.

"Hmm, my mother always called it lucky. What makes you say that?"

"Well, that it landed there and not on your face."

"Shawn!" He rolled his eyes and held a moment of tender silence before bursting into laughter.

Humor brought David closer. He didn't allow laughter to distance; he folded it in as if it were a key ingredient of attraction. I felt ease. I felt unencumbered, like I wasn't there to perform or fulfill a sexual checklist. We fell back into each other, and David knew how to support his partner's body. My lips moved over his soft bearded chin and slowly massaged their way down his neck and chest. I straddled his body. David took a deep breath, and the accordion of his ribs relaxed as I traveled over his pillowed navel.

"Stop!" He held my head in his hands and halted my advancement.

I froze. My hands hovered above my ears. David lifted my head, unsuctioning our bodies. I felt paused in a levitating magic act, awaiting further direction.

"We have to stop," he repeated.

"Absolutely." I slid off the bed, offering him space. "I'm sorry if I was moving too fast . . ."

"Oh GOD, no. You have to turn off the television. The curling is killing it for me."

I looked towards the flat-screen hanging on the wall and jumped into a panic just as Great Britain was about to throw the hammer in a pre-Olympic tournament round. "Shit!"

The light commentary had been droning in the background the entire time, and I hadn't even registered the noise. *You're more visual than auditory.* And I had been distracted by an extraordinary view: the contrast of David's even skin against a crisp white duvet. *David is sexy, curling is not.*

"Please make it stop!" David begged.

I looked to the bedside tables, the floor, and began to frantically flop naked around the hotel room searching for the remote. *Find the fucking remote! Don't ruin this! Where the fuck is it?*

"Turn it off!" David writhed on the bed, feigning pain. He laughed hard and loud as I failed to manually turn off the TV, searched desperately for the power source, then mimed ripping the television off the wall. David bubbled in joy. Then he maneuvered his hand under his backside and pulled out a remote stashed in the fold of the duvet. "Found it!"

With one click the crisis was over.

I don't know how (and I surprise even myself), but I have slept with some of the world's most beautiful men — symmetrical, chiseled, radiant. David looked at me unlike anyone I had ever been intimate with. To be the object of David's gaze was to feel the fullness of his life force. I stood naked, silent, erect, and without apology. I did not try to distract him from the years I've spent behind a computer, the freckles, the scars, the pastries. I didn't hide myself from him, and where I'd normally contract or deflate, my chest expanded so my shoulder blades kissed. My resting temperature raised a full degree as I began to thaw in front of a stranger who was no stranger. Though we had just met, I knew him. David stared deep into this knowing, my long-guarded barricade opened, and my depths flooded with sensation.

David shifted to kneel at the edge of the bed. Under his body weight, the duvet cupped his knees and the soft mattress dipped into the waters of desire.

"Come." He reached out to me.

The bed was a raft, and David pulled me from months — years, decades — of treading water alone. Face-to-face our torsos met, thighs burned, and our hardness rubbed in the soft flesh of our abdomens. We leaned in, leveraging the overlapping ropes of our arms with force as if trying to pull through one another. As sweat began to bead, the peel of our muscles slid and stretched to discover our curves and grooves.

The morning light flooded through the window facing east, clear of obstructions from the tight surrounding buildings. The

California sun crested above the city without its hard edge and illuminated everything with a shimmering gold translucence. David and I broke from each other to breathe in the effect. We smiled. It bathed David's sculpted face, filled the valleys of deep laugh lines, and refracted off his perfect teeth with the glimmer of precious metal. *This is the most beautiful man I've ever seen.* The light bathed my skin in warmth, shading in the definition of my muscles. *Nature's mercy.* We played in the flaxen iridescence, moving it with our bodies, letting it guide our mouths, lips, and hands until our breath was shallow, our pleasure was synced, and we could no longer withstand the effort of containing our orgasms. The noisy release left us panting, holding each other, while sweat and cum pooled and soaked into borrowed sheets.

"Oh wow! We could have been doing this the entire week," I said as my breath settled.

"I know," he said shaking his head.

David's iPhone alarm buzzed on the dark burgundy bedside table. "Oof, I should transition now." David reached to swipe off his alarm.

Transition?

I watched David rinse in the shower and helped him towel off. He reached towards my hair product on the chipped veneer countertop and silently asked if he could use my medium-hold paste. He unscrewed the tube and judged the citrus scent before working a small amount of white clay into his palm. He rolled his fingertips through his wavy black hair. He was due for a fresh cut, but the messiness worked.

"This is good," he said panning his chin left to check his profile. "Hmmm." My basic Canadian product met his exacting American standards. *This man is very particular.*

The sun was fully up, and we were fully dressed. David grabbed my hand and walked us slowly to the door. The electronic lock clicked open, and we moved to stand in the threshold.

"Oh! I forgot." I ran to the desk and back holding opened bags of Trader Joe's dried coconut strips in one hand and roasted unsalted cashews in the other. "As promised. Take one. Or both. As a parting gift?"

David looked at my offerings. He took several beats to weigh the snack foods before selecting the coconut strips.

"Seriously, not the cashews?"

He chuckled. He squished the coconut strips into the side pocket of his jacket. He wrapped his one hand to support my neck, the other hand pressed into my lower back. He leaned in for a long goodbye kiss, the type where you take breaks to rub foreheads or noses or rest the napes of necks into jawlines and breathe. While David and I transitioned, a white nuclear family, vacation ending, rolled their oversized luggage out of room 707 into the hall. The mother and father quickly shooed their kids towards the elevator, and David and I laughed, discovering that we had an audience to our most intimate affair. We didn't care. I felt proud to provide this family with a gay San Francisco moment.

"I've got to go." David broke away.

"Well . . . have a nice life?"

"Don't say that!" He winced before taking his first step away.

"David," I apologized, "I'm really bad at endings."

David smiled and walked down the hallway. I watched him leave from the doorway, indulging in the romantic farewell while balancing the practicality of not wanting to be locked out of my room without a key.

"David!"

He stopped and turned.

"Why do I feel like I'm going to see you very soon?"

David moved back towards me, grabbed me by the waist, and spun me back inside the hotel room. He pressed me against the inside of the door and whispered, "This is just the beginning." It would be another ten minutes before the door clicked open again and I watched David make his second attempt towards the elevator. I knew this would not be the last time I saw David. He gently waved so long (for now) every five or six steps until he rounded the corner of the hallway and disappeared (for now).

I showered, packed my remaining personal items into a duffel bag, and checked out of the Hotel Rex. With my black bag slung over my shoulder and clutching a half-eaten bag of cashews, I made my way towards the BART station. As my post-hookup high matured, my appreciation for San Francisco blossomed. It was a beautiful Friday morning, the skies were clear blue, the trolly dinged as it passed with tourists. My heart was swollen by the time I arrived at Market and Powell. I didn't want to leave. *But you hate San Francisco! Shh . . . it's got a red bridge, delightful sea lions, and moderate temperatures year-round.* David's cologne lingered on me. I felt fireflies in my chest. I'd fallen hard and fast. There was no second-guessing these feelings. In a city with so many rough edges to snag oneself on, I found myself attached to a charming, single, and emotionally available Californian.

Seventeen days later, we found each other at the arrivals gate of Toronto's Pearson International Airport and locked in a passionate kiss as families wheeled their oversized luggage around us.

"I told you I'd see you again," I said, resting my forehead on his.

"Let's get home as fast as possible."

I handed him a thick black winter parka. "Welcome to Canada."

We moved fast and fell hard over our devices after room 708. A signal connection on the BART meant that I could text with David en route to catch my flight. We added each other to socials by the time I passed through airport security, and I learned his last name. I posted a photo of my cashews, he posted his coconut strips, and we tagged each other. It was a public expression. We sprinkled these initial breadcrumbs of a relationship; months from now someone could scroll back to see the moment when two odd matches connected. The five-hour flight, the three thousand miles only strengthened desire. The time difference between Pacific and Eastern meant we had twenty-seven hours every day to ideate a relationship, sync our movements, snap photos of our vantage points, and share links that stirred us.

After David visited Toronto, we moved ever faster, and we stretched our deepest longings between two screens. We patched into each other's nervous system. A swipe of the glass interface on one end felt like fingertips caressing the forearm on the other; each message whispered warmly on the nape of the neck and surged blood to our faces, chests, and pelvises. David had a different relationship to time as if he could bend or extend the hours in a day. Time was no longer an objective measurement, a way to organize the day efficiently; I felt it as pulses of information flowing from one body to another and landing as big sensations.

The invention of the telegraph shifted the experience of time for the Victorians. Standardized time replaced local solar time (calculated by the midday sun), trains ran promptly on schedule, and messages from the empire's far reaches were sent and received instantly. A biological relationship to time crumbled as travel and communication sped faster, as bodies and information accelerated through space and over vast distances. The general public enjoyed the wonder of modern convenience and the awe of scientific advancement. In contrast, the telegraph operators experienced automation, relaying vast amounts of information at lightning speed. Did they feel a collapse of time and space in their bodies? Did they feel split between two places? In this era of rapid advancement, spiritualism and futurism arose: was that a coincidence or a by-product of radical change? If humans could channel electricity, control time, and condense space, why couldn't they commune with the past and predict the future?

The iPhone and the Android are the telegraphs of our time, and we are all operators bridging two realms: the physical and the digital. The digital can be a profoundly empathetic space where fantasy is bountiful and relationships move at the speed of connection. Love is both a matter of the heart and a bodily sixth, seventh, and eighth sense. You can feel synchronized with a lover on the opposite side of the world. You can walk on different terrains in different time zones, wishing your mate were beside you while their presence resonates in your body — as if they are. You can think of your love, then a message arrives in your pocket, and the timing of a thought with reciprocation opens the heart to metaphysical ideals of synchronicity. The assimilation stage of a fresh relationship becomes simulation, where the only difference between falling in love and feeling haunted is the promise of physical connection.

Putting touch on layaway is now the poetry of modern love.

Just grabbing a coffee.

Miss you.

Just in a meeting, but out in ten.

Have lunch in five.

How was the show?

Amazing.

Aw.

Wish you were there.

Wanna j/o together tonight?

Yes.

I wish you were in my bed.

Can't wait to feel you inside me.

April 2018

David and I relaxed in Precita Park, a long rectangle of lush grass outlined in mature blackwood acacia trees situated on the bottom north slope of Bernal Heights. The park spans several blocks and is bookended with a playground and café on the east side, a laundromat and bodega on the west. A long, cold winter wicked off my body, and my long-held tensions seeped deep down through layers of soil to be carried to the bay by the river that flowed underneath our bodies.

"This is perfect," David said.

"It is," I admitted.

Being in a park and dinner at six thirty — those were our major tasks for the day. Breakfast, sex, and coffee were already crossed off our to-do list.

David lay in the sunshine, listening to a podcast. My head rested on his chest. I rode the waves of his breath, up and down, while shading myself with the newspaper. Our bodies woven together, on public display. Above, a clear azure sky was marbled with white trails from planes flying overhead. My body sank further into David and the luxury of doing nothing. After years of grinding work and decades of nonstop ambition, I found myself pressing pause and giving in to the intense longing David revealed in me.

"Lean into my tree," David said in David-speak. "Let me be your tree trunk."

I sank deeper into my love.

David-speak was filled with turns of phrase that left me rethinking the meaning of words. Like *transition*: where most of us would curse and hurry, David *transitioned*, moving from one state to another with grace, an awareness of movement, and complete presence. He created contexts for words outside their normal usage. There was a consideration to his language, and his precision fostered my curiosity. At times I found it overwhelmingly frustrating, most often I found it romantic. Understanding the poetry of David was the major hurdle, other than physical distance, to us being together.

"You're not here!" David shouted.

Our frustrations crested on the shores of Ocean Beach. The winds were especially dramatic that first morning on the West Coast as we winced against the harsh grains of sand that pelted our skin. We stood in a no-man's land of white noise, between a curving high tide of frigid Pacific water crashing on land and traffic whooshing through a thick fog on the Great Highway.

"What?"

"You're not *here*."

"Am I invisible?" I pulled at the skin on my face. "David, can you see me?"

"Yes, I can see you. But you're not present. You're tied up somewhere in the past."

I needed the water to surge, for the dangerous riptide to grab our conversation by the feet and pull it out to the horizon. I stared at David, hurt by his words. We were learning how to fight as someone's off-leash Shiba Inu circled, happy and oblivious to our awkward couple moment and unfazed by the blustery day. David was exacting in his observations, and his criticisms paralyzed me. But the source of his frustration was unclear, and feeling as if I had offended him, I played back everything I had done or said since I landed at the airport. I'd flown three thousand miles to be with him. I was physically there. Was I present? I had no idea what David meant, and I didn't feel like confronting a Buddhist existential crisis while on an extended holiday. Jet-lagged and worn-out from a run of performances and hosting gigs, I needed a moment to sit on a beach, listen to some waves, and indulge in the access and excess that Californians take for granted. David wanted to dive deep into relational work.

"I'm worried we're on different paths."

"David, I'm not a philosopher. But you're never on the same path as someone. Sometimes paths run parallel, sometimes they weave in and out, sometimes one path ends before another. This is life."

"I need someone who can show up for me."

"I don't understand."

"Can you show up? Be here?"

"Yes. I'm here. I'm beside a man I love. I'm present because I can feel shards of sand giving me a much-needed microdermabrasion facial."

David laughed. Laughter broke his intensity, it allowed for him to register his surroundings. "You love me?"

"I do. And you?"

"I love you too."

"My feelings have feelings," said David.

"I'm learning this."

Our heads met and we mended our frustrations with an apologetic kiss. It wasn't the first time we'd professed our love, but it was the first time we had in person. We'd constructed our relationship online and studied how to be together, but we needed time to practice the realities of being together, and that required patience. Patience was not one of David's virtues. During his Toronto visit, David had given me a large blue marble, a talisman to hold. It was a representation of what we were building together; he called it "the bubble." Merging with one another while maintaining the bubble was like the shortened ramps to the freeways that bordered Bernal — it demanded a heavy foot on the gas and trust that every moving piece would align and not collide.

After our fight on the beach, David and I cooled our emotions by climbing the summit of Bernal Hill. Encircled by a mile-long path of crushed red rock, sand, and asphalt, the steady incline revealed a panoramic view of the San Francisco skyline. At the top, I could see from Sutro Tower to the Bay Bridge and as deep as the Golden Gate Bridge and the Marin Headlands. We sat side by side, with our legs overlapped, and picked at the long grass. A coyote appeared on a hillock several yards away from us. The lone trickster, whose infamy and likeness I'd seen posted on warning signs on the climb up, ventured from its den and watched us. Harmless, the carrion-eater made its presence known and then vanished. We were awestruck, and with our bodies grounded on millions of tons of compressed quartz, we went full woo-woo.

We interpreted the coyote as an omen of our good fortune together, and agreed then and there that we were yesses for each other.

We fell into an easy rhythm on Bernal Hill; David and I trekked to the summit daily (sometimes twice) to sit on the rocky slopes and watch the sun rise or set. Some evenings we were escorted by Ziggy, the roaming black cat of Alabama Street, who led us to the entrance of the park. Some mornings Rachael, David's city mom, accompanied us. I would listen to the two lovingly discuss politics and freelancing between offerings of book reviews and slow cooker recipes. Bernal Hill was a natural refuge, a preserved ecosystem of wildflowers, orange poppies, tall grasses, hawks, and owls. A microclimate of warm air pushed down the hill's leeward face to a charming village decorated with lush succulent beds, magenta bougainvilleas, and tuna plants bearing ripe prickly pears.

David and I wrapped up our afternoon in Precita and headed home to take a nap before family dinner at Rachael's. We climbed the steady slope of Alabama to a side street, then vaulted over the latest Amazon deliveries blocking the front door, then up the first flight of stairs to the kitchen. David stopped and grabbed a bottle of seltzer fresh from his beloved SodaStream and three protein bars. David and I overheard exaggerated laughter and grating baby talk from the living room. We climbed the steps to the second landing and interrupted a pleasure party. On the sectional couch sat one of David's roommates, half dressed in a drugstore adult Princess Jasmine costume. Topless, breasts exposed, she was flanked by two clothed butch slaves who teased her hard nipples with faux fur and feathers.

"I forgot to tell you I was having a tickle party," Princess Jasmine squeaked in a baby voice. "Feel free to stay and watch."

David grabbed my hand and pulled me towards the next staircase.

After his breakup, David had moved off his friend's couch into a shared housing situation. We nicknamed it the Sex-Positive Home after the craigslist ad title David had answered. The cost was outrageous (apparently affordable for San Francisco), and the roommate setup proved problematic. The towering split-level '90s remodeled home was owned by Princess Jasmine, a thirty-something musical theatre performer and self-identified hugger. After her parents exited the Bay Area, Jasmine transformed her childhood home into a rooming house and pleasure dome. David paid two thousand dollars a month to live in the top floor master suite. David's space was a private chalet sitting above madness. White walls, vaulted ceilings, bleached wood furniture, and through the cathedral windows you could see the communication tower on Bernal Hill. He shared the kitchen and common areas with four roommates: Princess Jasmine, two who worked in tech, and one who dressed as a pirate. The pirate was the sexual convener and would send emails advising of body painting sessions and upcoming play parties in the living room. The unannounced tickle party broke the communication ethos that everyone who stayed over in the Sex-Positive Home had to read and agree to. The whole situation reminded me of the over-sexed geeks in high school who fucked like rabbits despite their position in the social strata.

David didn't fit amongst his housemates, and there were ongoing tensions between him and Princess Jasmine, mostly passive-aggressive emails back and forth concerning his cologne or laundry detergent. Jasmine was scent sensitive and constantly clocking the moisture levels for her vocal cords. It was neurosis and control disguised as allergies. If she left the house, which was seldom, she wore an N95 mask to protect her voice, but the ground floor reeked of mold and mildew from the dozen or more rotting bouquets in vases filled with putrid brown water. A large aquarium sat in the corner filled with stagnant water, algae climbing over its edges. Amazon boxes cluttered the floor while the cupboards were filled with reusable mason jars and aluminum water bottles. The back patio was a field of shit bombs from a three-legged Chihuahua, a trihuahua, who sneaked through a hole in the fence to relieve himself. Jasmine was meant to manage the home, but it was becoming clearer that the roommates were paying for her shut-in lifestyle by living around her and not with her.

I looked at David as we reached the fifth-floor landing, trying not to laugh or comment.

"Don't say it." David broke out in massive giggles. "I know exactly what you're thinking."

"I'm not saying anything."

"But?"

"No buts."

"What about this one?" David said, slapping my ass.

"Do we have time before dinner?"

"Oh, we've got time."

He shut the door to his bedroom, muffling Princess Jasmine's performance. He pulled me in close and our lips connected.

We quickstepped towards the bed as we tore off our clothes, parting only to pull our T-shirts over our heads. David pushed me onto the mattress and peeled off my pants and underwear. He stretched his arm for the bottle of lubricant on the bedside table. He snapped open the lid and poured a generous stream of slippery silicone onto his hardness, then passed the half-empty bottle to me. *It was full when you arrived.* David hooked my left leg over his shoulder; the blades of my back dug into the duvet as he lifted and carried the weight of my lower body onto his hips. He rocked his pelvis and my hands drifted over his face, chest, his working biceps, my hardness. I noticed my hands more in the new world of preventative HIV meds. Instead of reaching down to inconspicuously feel for the band of a condom, they explored my partner's body without worry. There was no double, triple, quadruple checks. No monitoring for stealthing. David was the first man to ever be inside me without a barrier. There was no separation between us as our bodies glided together on molecules of sweat and spit and lube. David's spine arched over my body, and his hair painted sweat across my forehead. I could smell his natural scent through his fading cologne. I took all of him deep inside me, explored my birthright to pleasure, to my body. To finally claim agency over my body felt like a luxury not experienced in decades, the gay love story transformed from one of danger to one of passion. Trust was now a love language of daily check-ins to remind each other to take a large blue pill.

Rachael and her husband, John, lived one block north, on Boise Street. Their quaint navy-blue family home was at the foot of a thirty-one-and-a-half-percent grade. The Boise hill was frequented by skateboarders for amusement and adapted by personal trainers for torture. The head-on view of the slope offers a nauseating funhouse experience, a warped perspective of parallel-parked cars on the razor's edge of their tires and garbage bins that defy gravity. The otherwise quiet residential street sings with overworked engines, grating clutches, squeaking brakes both up and down.

"Their neighbors must be goats," I said to David.

"Ah-ha. Yup." He giggled. "Goat people."

"Just kid-ding."

David rolled his eyes, then burst into laughter.

You two are so annoying.

I could have used my own set of cloven hooves to trek these streets; even on a slight incline, my calves burned. David lightly swung a canvas bag filled with a bottle of wine from the park corner store and secret dessert from Canada. I carried a potted orange dahlia for Rachael, a thank-you for the handful of Meyer lemons she'd given me from her garden. We purchased the dahlia plant at a Pescadero goat farm on our last day trip down the coast — the reason we had goats on our brains.

"Here — you give it to Rachael."

"Me?" He grew awkward.

"Yes, you."

"Are you sure?"

"Absolutely."

David blushed in the way one glows in embarrassment walking down the street carrying a bouquet of flowers for a secret someone. David didn't often show his bashful nature; he softened with animals, plants, and food. We stood at the foot of a long terrazzo staircase, and I leaned over and kissed him. The bright turmeric-colored door opened before our feet hit the first stair. This was Rachael and John's generosity of spirit: the door always swung open before there was time to knock.

Rachael's wavy golden blonde hair was in a loose ponytail, her full bangs met the top ridge of her arched brows, and she wore her reading glasses as a headband and dangly chandelier earrings. John tucked his jaw-length hair behind his ears; its silver tone accented his olive skin. They smiled with genuine enthusiasm and joy for life, and they appeared to enjoy a sense of ease entering retirement. Rachael was an executive coach and maintained a busy volunteering schedule at school or as a community whip for the Democratic party. John was retired, and he spent his days writing historical novels and occasionally ushered concerts and sports games at night. The home was a museum of a happy family; it lovingly chronicled the raising of their daughter, the pets (loved and lost), the souvenirs from their vacations. It wasn't a sterile show home but well worn, cozy, and eclectic. It was tailored to the activities they loved: a breakfast nook for drinking espresso with warm milk, a gray armchair by the window for reading the *New York Times* cover to cover, a built-in polytheistic wall altar, a lush garden of perennial flowers and vegetables, and a large dining room table for dinner parties. The couple instantly made you jealous that you weren't related and couldn't live in their basement.

"Does anyone want a little vino?" Rachael said, pulling a chilled bottle of white from the fridge.

"I'll take some," said David, who seldom indulged in alcohol.

The wine was poured, the dining table was set, and we broke bread over slow-cooked pulled pork, roasted artichoke hearts from the garden, and warm kimchi pancakes. We were surrounded by an extensive collection of books displayed on orange shelves — both food and words were nourishment in the Boise home. Conversation was the key ingredient and we all shared the same taste in humor and love of wordplay. I savored the couple's historical knowledge of their neighborhood: that it was the only area not devastated by the 1906 earthquake, that the hill is formed of tectonically folded Franciscan chert and is unshakeable from base to peak, and the summit was saved in the '60s by community organizers.

There was such curiosity about my being Canadian, and the couple flexed their knowledge of my home and native land: old episodes of *SCTV*, media hits on Trudeau's socks, and the many times John turned off the radio when Céline Dion came on. I'd brought butter tarts from my favorite bakery in Ontario — six frozen mini sugar pies with raisins and pecans that thawed on the plane until they found their way into David's fridge. I explained the cultural significance of the gooey pastries as a staple for baby showers and funerals, or as a serotonin replacement during the winter. David and I inhaled ours, Rachael and John marveled at the sugar content.

"What's the most significant difference between our two countries?" asked John.

"Other than universal healthcare? Lemons."

I am a passionate person when it comes to produce, and I let loose Julia Child hysterics when Rachael told me to pick fresh citrus in her backyard. Lemon trees were my most startling revelation about California, where I noticed a gap in my understanding gleaned from Hollywood iconography. Lemons weren't a three-for-two-dollar buy at the grocery store, they were free and in abundance. With those margins and the right acumen, a child could turn a profit with an artisanal lemonade stand in California. I grew up with four apple trees in my backyard, but never once tried to sell apple juice for twenty-five cents a glass. My enthusiasm for citrus was exhausting, but it seemed like an endearing quirk that was goaded at the table.

"Lemons!" Rachael laughed. "Well, who knew?"

Nothing in this scenario was foreign to me; I understood it intimately: the politics and puns, the intellectual and the silly, the telling and the making of stories, the wine and more wine. All of it reminded me of the dinners I've spent with my chosen family in Toronto, the Bloomfields. Every Sunday, unless I was traveling or natural disaster prevented us from gathering, I broke bread with a family who invited me to their table as if I were their own. I was flabbergasted to discover a parallel experience, but in a warmer climate. Rachael and John were interchangeable with Louisa and her late husband, George. I understood why David tolerated the absurdity of his rental situation: to be close to a family he considered his own.

"So Shawn," John edged on teasing. "Tell me your thoughts on this Sex-Positive Home."

"Well . . . I'm not there to judge . . ." I said between gulps of wine.

"But?" lobbed Rachael.

"But I'm also not there to participate."

Laughter erupted.

"Should I tell them about Princess Jasmine?" offered David.

"Hold on, I'll get some more wine and some dark chocolate," said Rachael.

David and I returned home with leftovers of pulled pork, two mason jars of homemade granola, and fistfuls of lemons. Rachael invited us over for coffee and breakfast in the morning before our four-hour hike in Point Reyes to Alamere Falls, a rare tide fall of freshwater that cascades over rock and flows into the Pacific. David and I ended our day with a long hot bath in the soaker tub and listening to an episode of *On Being*. We stood naked on a private rooftop balcony and toweled each other off. The cold night air kissed our warm flesh as steam curled in the street light. David held me from behind as we looked out over the Mission.

"Remember Cesar Chaves divides the Mission from Bernal." David pointed.

He pressed himself into me and kissed the back of my neck.

David held an enormous appetite, not just for food and sex. Yes, he could eat four hamburgers in one sitting and have sex multiple times a day, but his insatiable libido for life was magnetic. In me, a hunger beyond career or ambition stepped to the forefront. I had starved myself for years, withholding my desires, restricting my experience. My blossoming pointed to a deficit, and I wanted in on the West Coast lifestyle. I didn't need a pair of high-waisted palazzo pants to explore my coyote appetites for food, nature, laughter, and especially sex. I wished to roll out of bed three hours later than the entire East Coast, to feast on vegan donuts, lap up creamy horchata, and wolf down Mission burritos. I craved biodiversity in a temperate climate filled with raptors and docile Pomeranians. I lusted for the ocean. I desired a perennial garden of honeycomb dahlias, artichokes, and lemons.

I yearned for more.

My wet skin constricted against the chill in the night air. I felt David grow hard against my back.

I yearned for more with him.

I met Eros at a crossroads, halfway between breaking up with Matt and meeting David.

"This way," he said.

Before discovering California, I found myself in Quebec. Stock Bar was a rite of passage for Toronto gays — a formality repeated on each weekend escape to Montreal. The club was slow for a Friday night, or maybe we'd arrived early. I sat with three friends. We drank bottles of Labatt 50 and ate free popcorn while watching the acts. The energy of the cabaret did not match the hype of the mumbling emcee who introduced the performers who danced or showered for money. It was a limp night for everyone in the club.

François was shorter than the other dancers, but his physique was perfection to me. He was compact and proportional, unlike the taller, stretched-out exotic dancers who gyrated in red Adidas track pants to Britney Spears's "Gimme More" or masturbated artfully to Leonard Cohen's "Hallelujah." I called him François because that was the name tattooed across his shoulder blades, arcing in a serif font like a letterman jacket. His name could have been Marc, Jeffrey, or Ryan — I had encountered Eros many times in my life.

When François approached the line of cocktail tables, he was fishing for a transaction, someone to join him on the other side of the velvet curtains for a private dance for twenty dollars a song. He wore a black tank top and a pair of light-wash skinny jeans.

"Any of you interested in a dance tonight?"

He walked down the line being rejected friend by friend until he stood in front of me. I could have ignored him, but I didn't. The amount of times that had happened to me as a performer, that someone looked right through me instead of seeing me — I could never harm someone in that way. I, too, rejected François's offer. I felt as if I had a few decades left before I paid for the attention of men.

"I don't feel like working tonight," François admitted.

"Tough crowd?"

"Yup. Can I sit with you?"

"Of course."

Instead of a dance, we talked.

François was a novice in the club, without the status of the other performers. He admired his coworkers for their pole-dancing skills, the discipline they put into their bodies, and the money they made to care for their families. He was saving up to buy a pair of G-Star RAW jeans — I gleaned that the heavy wash brand with ornate decorations was a hyperlocal trend among the employees of Stock Bar. François feared his girlfriend didn't like him because his penis was small and she spoke unkindly to him. His tattoo was in memory of someone he loved. He debated whether or not he should finish his degree or enter a trade. For now, he split his nights between the cabarets of Montreal, dancing for both women and men — his girlfriend preferred him to dance for men.

He relaxed as our conversation got thicker and I offered my own story. I told him about how I'd buried myself in work after my relationship with Matt ended ten months ago and that I had a book coming out. I talked around my ascetic lifestyle, about self-discipline and working hard to fix the factors that caused my breakup. Forty minutes later, I caught myself feeling guilty, like I was preventing him from finding a high-paying client. When the host mumbled his name in the microphone, François reluctantly ran across the club and backstage.

François removed his shirt as he walked onstage and stood in my direct eyeline. He began to dance, shifting his weight side-to-side in a slow meditation, twisting the snake of his spine and sinking into his pelvis, finding moments of effort and relaxation between beats in the music. François understood movement as a language. He wasn't performing choreography but having a silent conversation with his audience. What he was saying with his body was up for interpretation, but that he was saying something vital was undeniable. François locked eyes with me and did not break his focus. I could feel my face getting flushed. When his song ended, he came directly back to my table. He grabbed me by the hand and pulled me out of my chair.

"I want to dance for you."

"I'm not the type —"

"I don't care. I want to dance for you."

"Don't judge me," I mouthed to my friends as I walked away.

François held my hand like we were on a first date as he led me to the private area by the right side of the stage. He sat me on a gray vinyl padded bench and pulled a privacy curtain closed. The lighting was dim and the space was cramped. I watched him kick off his shoes, pull off his pants, and neatly fold them. He slipped his sneakers back on and inched himself close to me. He clamped the outside of my knees with the inside of his legs, putting his groin at my eye level. He began his dance by caressing my face.

"Touch me."

I tentatively placed my hands on either side of his hip bones like a steering wheel.

"No, touch me. Grab my flesh. Feel me."

I dug my hands into his muscles. His skin was soft, and he smelled like coconut oil. François got hard and slid his underwear down to his knees; the stretched waistband of his Calvin Kleins locked our legs together. François was deeply rooted in his body; my body mirrored that depth. As one song faded into another, he led me deeper into the abyss of my own flesh. Then Heart's "Alone" began to play on the speaker system — the cosmos had offered my all-time favorite band. With François's body moving in the dim light and Ann Wilson's fierce siren's call in the ether, a Montreal lap dance was elevated to religious experience. My breath dropped, my blood pumped through my body, I looked up at François backlit with a crown of light.

The word *desire* means to await what the stars will bring.

When the song ended, François started to dress. "Was that okay?"

"That was beautiful," I said, spellbound. "What do I owe you?"

"Nothing. I wanted to be with you."

I pulled forty dollars from my wallet. "This isn't for the dance, but for your new jeans. From artist to artist."

He smiled and accepted the bills from my hand. I liked how his bottom teeth were crooked. "I like how you talk to me."

"And I like how you spoke to me, François."

"You know my name is not François, right?"

"I know."

"Can I hug you?" he softy asked.

We stood and held each other by the exit of the private rooms.

"Your lover is wrong about the size of your dick," I told him.

He laughed and we broke apart.

We overlook the healing nature of pleasure and of grounded touch. The dance was a conversation about power, tenderness, sex, and vulnerability between two male bodies without any shame, judgment, or punishment. François spoke to me like the wind that sighs on the edge of a sail and entices it in a new direction, just ever so slightly. *This way.* He danced from a place of abundance, as if there was an infinite universe behind him. For the length of three songs, I reconnected to pleasure and remembered that I have a body. I left Stock Bar swirling from the kindness of our exchange.

June 3, 2018

Stop managing personalities. Stop controlling your experience with others. All you can do is make invitations. You create a container for people to show up and to be their best selves. If people are assholes, they're assholes. It's YOUR birthday!

I coached myself with some hard talk to quell the cold anxiety sweat of my immediate situation. I looked around at the various factions of my life in one space. My oldest friends from high school mingled with my newest. My baby mamas, Teresa and Rita, chatted with my close gay male friends. Louisa, my city mom, found the French or Italian speakers in the room and dug deep into her first and third languages. Daccia, my faux sister, helped me play host. Greta, my six-year-old kid, made herself known to all the adults. My male friends met my daughter for the first time. Straight mixed with gay, and everyone magically enjoyed themselves. It appeared to be a casual act to just blend them all, but for me it was a radical act of vulnerability. I let go of the weight of holding up social barriers and allowed my worlds to collapse in my living room for this occasion.

One person was absent: Matt, my ex–common law husband. For years, we hosted beautiful games nights, dinners, drunken kitchen parties, and holiday celebrations for our different pockets of friends in our little city apartment. It was bountiful, and we were never without company, but we always kept the various groups separate. He became my co-captain, my wingman as we traveled from world to world (both his and mine). Life was easier with an ally at these events, someone who also understood the intricacies and backstories of our chosen family trees.

I saw Louisa surveying the guests and the flow of the party. She wore a designer crinoline party dress, bijoux, and bangles, with her blonde hair perfectly blown out. Louisa's youthful effervescence and style defied her age as she enjoyed her seventies with flair.

"You didn't want to invite Matt?" Louisa asked. "It's a shame he's missing this."

The fantasy narrative of a Matt and Shawn reunion ensnared me still. Most people held out hope for the plot resolution of a wedding. I still carried the weight of blame while trying to move on, as if I bore the sole responsibility for our breakup. Matt still attended our weekly Sunday dinners, but he'd naturally weaned himself away from all other connections. I was finally, whole-heartedly attempting to move forward alongside someone new. It was important to me that my community met the person who had captured my heart and sparked my personal renaissance, even if that meant buying my own birthday cake and throwing myself a party.

"Matt left me two years ago, Louisa. He didn't want this. Today is about introducing David to everyone."

The Bloomfields had taken on the tough challenge of reparenting me when I first moved to Toronto. Louisa was a chef and surrealist painter, and George was a venerable director of Canadian film and television who continued to work well into his eighties. Through affluence and with generosity, Louisa had taught me the practice of abbondanza, the Italian word for abundance or plenty. Over two decades of Sunday night dinners, I learned the unsubtle art of celebrating. It was an education through weekly feasts where champagne flutes bubbled over and four-finger shots of bourbon were poured between courses of prime cuts of meat roasted to perfection and decadent buttercream topped cakes. Abbondanza is the art of finding any excuse to cheers, to break bread, even over the minute events of life.

I mirrored Louisa's spirit, the way she expresses her love, and went overboard with my taco birthday party theme. I wore taco socks and authentic papel picado was strung across the living room (gifts from Rachael and John, direct from San Francisco's Mission District). The bright tissue-paper bunting matched the balloons kicking around the floor; green saguaro cactus candles were embedded in pots of orange and yellow marigolds and placed around the house and lit. I wanted my community to savor the flavors of the Mission that made my mouth water. The apartment smelled of slow-roasted pork shoulder carnitas served with sliced radishes, jalapeños, and limes. Vats of fresh salsa verde and guacamole, pitchers of homemade horchata, hand-squeezed lime margaritas, and ice-cold cerveza signaled a fiesta for an entire building. I was winded from the preparation, but it felt critical to make a statement. I used abbondanza to show David everything, no bluffing or hiding.

I watched David leaning in the doorway to the living room as he surveyed everyone around him. He watched as clusters of friends formed throughout the apartment, broke apart, and then reformed in beautiful ways. He didn't attempt to introduce himself as Greta whizzed by his feet chasing a balloon. The setting was a lot to take in — even for me. I still couldn't believe that the child running room-to-room was the same baby I helped my friends Teresa and Rita to conceive by acting as a sperm donor. This vibrant, laughing, talking, walking human was my greatest joy. But I sensed David judging my world, and that filled me with a wave of disappointment. I looked at David and smiled, offering my support. He struggled to smile back. I didn't know this David. I wanted to go over and introduce myself, spark a casual conversation, ask him about his career, where he was born, and how he knew the host. He expertly played the role of an unwanted guest, but everyone around him (except maybe Louisa) held an excitement about this man who was calling me to California.

For two people living three thousand miles apart, over the last four months we'd managed to go no more than fifteen days without physical contact. Only ten days had passed since we'd last seen each other. In that time apart David had boxed up his room in the Sex-Positive Home, placed his life in two storage units, and got a sublet on the south side of Bernal for July and August. June, he planned to explore our relationship while working remotely from Toronto — perfect timing, since the city had shaken the persistent flu of winter and blossomed into summer. David scheduled a return layover in LA to visit friends and to scout the city for a potential move that included me. I would make two separate treks to California over the summer to be with him. It was a lot of coordinating, and our plans were working.

But David had arrived like a stranger at the airport. He walked from the gate tugging on a gigantic wheeled bag that was big enough for an overseas trek on a 1920s ocean liner. He appeared tired, guarded, and defeated. This time he was the one not present. Where was the romantic who called in the early hours of the morning, who sexted, who plotted a future with me?

Who is this man?

A viola appeared in the hand of a musician friend and everyone sang "Happy Birthday," on key and in harmony — a miracle. I sat on the blue sofa with Greta clasped between my legs, and together we blew out the candles on my cake. David migrated from the doorway to sit next to me. Louisa cut the cake, and Greta delivered slices to everyone in the room. I expressed my joy for a year of hard work, the gifts of a successful book, for finding a new love, and for the discovery of California. The room congealed and everyone squeezed around the coffee table and the stories both new and old started coming out: the absurd folktales of Shawn Hitchins were shared. Laughter erupted and David came to life. He finally arrived for my friends and family. I looked at David, hoping that this would be the last year I purchased my own birthday cake. He looked back at me with an electric smile. This was the man I knew and loved.

The next morning, David and I chilled in the living room drinking cold brew and talking about the various things I wanted to do for my birthday. David sprung from the sofa, left the room, and re-entered with a card in his hand. He presented it to me.

"What's this?" I asked coyly.

"It's your gift!"

David straddled my thighs, his knees digging into the cushions of the sofa. He watched me open the envelope. The card was a small piece of watercolor paper folded in half with "Shew" written on the front. Inside was his elegant handwriting alongside a comical drawing of me. David offered me his wishes for the year ahead along with an offer: a marriage proposal. "A co-created California adventure" — David-speak for "Will you marry me?" He beamed as I read, interpreted, then reread his proposal. I didn't need a ring offered from a man on one knee, and I certainly didn't need another year to know my answer. I could see myself living with David in California, legally married.

"I do," I said.

"Yes?"

"Of course. Absolutely I will co-create a California adventure with you, David Martinez."

Our bodies fell into each other and we kissed in confirmation. *Okay, you're getting married? Don't fuck this up.* David felt my excitement bulging in my jogging pants.

"Let's shower," he whispered in my ear.

He led me to the bathroom, flung open the shower curtain, and turned on the water. We stripped out of our comfy jersey knits and stood naked under a stream of hot water. Unfortunately, shower sex in an apartment-sized tub means rotisserie-ing your bodies in and out of hot water. I steadied myself against the small window ledge, knocking over shampoo bottles. Hot water trickled over David's shoulders and landed on my chilled back, sporadic and distracting. The small room overfilled with steam, and I lost myself — not in the passion, but the disorienting fog. He rocked his pelvis until he suddenly yelped in pain and seized.

"My back!" David cried while still inside me.

I froze. "Shit! Okay! What should I do?"

"Keep going! I'm almost there!"

Keep going? Oh! Keep going!

I thrust my hips twice in reverse and David came, pleasure chased by pain. I toweled him off, slipped his underwear over his hips, and laid him down on the living room floor. When you're almost forty, shower sex becomes a hazard. David sank his body-weight into the floor and massaged the flesh of his lower back into the hardwood with circular motions. Years of professional dancing had brought wear and tear on his hips, knees, and lower back. He slept with a sandbag on each hip flexor to get him through the night.

Balloons bobbed around him in the breeze from the open apartment windows; he looked like he was floating in a sea. He breathed deep in and out as his back tightened more and more. I watched him disappear before my eyes.

"I need a doctor," the Stranger said.

David circled the living room, walking slowly, moving his hips in tiny circles with gentle bends in his knees. We'd returned from an emergency appointment with an osteopath down the street. In the two hours since I eased him out of the shower, an anger had swelled in David.

"We can't get married."

I laughed. "What? I know the shower sex wasn't amazing."

"I'm serious, we can't do this."

"We don't have to get married."

"It's over."

"Wait? Are you fucking breaking up with me on my birthday?"

"You don't know until you know."

"You don't know until you know?" I repeated slowly so that he could hear the curtness of his own words. "So why did you give me a card with a proposal?"

"I didn't know until now."

None of this makes sense. One minute you're engaged and fucking in a shower, the next it's over?

David pulled his phone out of his pocket and texted his friend Loren in Florida. He grabbed a set of housekeys and his headphones and waddled to the front door. He needed space, but space came with the discomfort of navigating four flights of stairs in an old deco walk-up. Two minutes later he waddled out the front door of my building and stood in the middle of the cul-de-sac, deep in conversation with Loren. I just watched him from a harsh angle through my living room window as he made circular motions with his hips and grand gestures with his hands. *What did you do?* Except a few comments back and forth over David's social media, I didn't know Loren, but I was invited to her wedding in September. She was a professional dancer, David's main support, his best friend since college. David often quoted her in conversation. They didn't go a day without long check-ins over the phone. I felt like I knew her. *Surely this will pass.*

"You lied to me," David said, entering the apartment.

"I did no such thing."

"You lied. You were never planning to move to me."

"David, we are only beginning the immigration conversation."

"You have four weeks to move to California!"

"What?" I laughed.

"I'm serious."

The living room looked hungover, strewn with free-range balloons and streamers. I scanned my furniture, my quirky collection of vintage finds, and the freshly painted walls. I saw the work I'd done to redo the space after Matt left. This was my home. A decade of my life had happened in this apartment. It was my creative and emotional nest. I'd written all my shows and my first book at the wooden kitchen table. I'd grieved George, Louisa's husband, on the blue couch. I'd sobbed in the foyer when Matt left. I'd experienced a roller-coaster of life and, through it all, this apartment was my stability. Yesterday the square footage was crowded with love and community, but today it felt restrictive. I was surrounded by stories, and I felt rootbound by them; I needed to grow, a place to start over, and someone to share that journey with. I looked at David and the rawness of his emotions and his physical discomfort. He was the only thing that mattered; possessions could all be shipped or sold, friends and family could fly down. I would give it all up for our big California life together.

"Fine, I'll get my green card."

"It's too late."

"What?"

"I told you it's over."

"So are you leaving?"

"Do you want me to leave?"

"I love you. I want you to stay and work through this confusion."

"I would like to stay."

"Is this because you have no other place to go?"

"No. Because I still love you. I want to be with you."

"And have sex?"

"Of course."

"You make no sense!" I hollered. "But you can stay, and we will have sex."

I took a steak knife from the butcher block and hunted the balloons, tore down the bunting. The party was over.

David changed his flight, shortening our time together to just another week; he stayed, but so did the Stranger. Day after day, the two characters grew more distinct; they tagged each other in and out. When David was present, we continued our relationship as we watched *Jane the Virgin*, cooked meals, worked side by side, wandered the city, and explored our bodies between the sheets. But then the Stranger would materialize out of nowhere to chastise or criticize my smallest action, wrong word, or touch. He was distant, cold, and unpredictable. I addressed the Stranger like a spirit in the room, a malevolent entity possessing David: "I don't know who is speaking, but when you say this to me, it feels unloving and hurts." I conjured, I summoned David, who would then reliably reappear.

The Stranger hated Toronto. He spent hours walking from store to store, shop to shop declaring Toronto a city "without pants." But David needed pants — he had worn through the seat of his favorite pair. David had needs, yet the Stranger offered no comfort or care or relief to him. In my emotional exhaustion, Toronto's pantlessness became my own failure. I needed David to see there were thousands of pairs of pants available to him. None were good enough for the Stranger. *You and your city's pants are not good enough.*

~ ~

"I think it's time I told you my story." One morning in bed, David looked at me with tears in his eyes, a parting in the confusion. The breaking news of Kate Spade's death by suicide followed so soon by Anthony Bourdain's broke his disposition.

"Tell me your story." I placed my hand in his.

David told me about his two failed attempts at suicide at the ages of nineteen and twenty-nine; his diagnosis of psychogenic seizures, the non-epileptic incidents that physically shook and rattled his body; his lifesaving diagnosis by a New York doctor named Siddhartha; his boyfriends who'd stood by him, and those who had not. I had collected his stories in bits and pieces from our conversations. I had my own experience with childhood difficulty, abuse, being on the margins, but it was the entirety of his story. It broke my heart. David's genius, his duende, even the Stranger that overtook him did not scare me. I grew up in a home that centered on a parent around whose emotional extremes I acquiesced to. Yes, David came with a price, but he was worth it.

I got up from the bed and walked over to my supply of yellow legal pads that I keep for my writing. I grabbed a fresh one from the middle of the stack and a fancy black pen. I handed both to him. "Write at my kitchen table," I said. "It's where I've done my best work." The rest of the day he sat writing a meditation on mental health and suicide. He then posted his message to Instagram along with a throwback portrait of him in New York, with his slogan, "The Future Is Feeling." The post was a daring public acknowledgment of his complex past, and it felt defiant on a platform that trades in the illusion of perfection. He spent the rest of the week expanding on his story and folding it into his statement for the coaching career he was launching. He gave me drafts, and I read them between emails and signing contracts with an immigration lawyer. When the Stranger popped in to visit, he didn't stay long; David's energy had shifted, and we found laughter again.

On our last day together, David and I caught the final minutes of brunch service at a popular diner in midtown. We sat in the back of Uncle Betty's at a four-top table by a large window. David lifted his coffee mug from the saucer. After his first sip of coffee, he smiled a wide but relaxed smile, and his eyes were filled with kindness. He wore his Levi's jean jacket and a pale bluish-gray T-shirt, his hair was perfectly set, and I could smell his cologne, Thé Noir 29 by Le Labo, from across the table. He reminded me of our first early morning date at Sears Fine Food. He was perfectly lit from the side. I picked up my iPhone and snapped a couple of portraits; one became my favorite photo of David. After so much tearing and mending it was miraculous to capture him in a moment of ease, suspended in time like a whale breeching from water. David then took my photo in the same light. In it I look tired, exhausted, and contemplative — his visit had put me through the emotional ringer. It is not my favorite photo taken by David.

That night we sat on the couch watching Pixar's *Coco*, then more episodes of *Jane the Virgin*. We got into a friendly debate about who was more like which character, similar to those inane conversations gay men of a certain age have about *Sex and the City* archetypes. *You are clearly the writer Jane, and David is the reformed bad boy Rafael*. David got absorbed into the telenovela, and he passionately explained the tropes of the genre: characters coming back to life, love triangles, cheating, passionate kisses, past criminal lives, ridiculous fights, and shocking deaths. I debated what was more enjoyable, watching the show or watching David watch his stories — he was dialed in to the experience. He wrapped his arm around me, and I sat close, cross-legged with his torn pants on my lap. David was embarrassed that he didn't have a pair of pants to wear in LA. The seat of his pants had finally ripped lengthways from the beltline to the lower left pocket on our way home from brunch. As we watched *Jane*, I hand-sewed a patch using a swatch of fabric cut from an old pair of my pants and a tight whipstitch. I reinforced the graft of cloth with an even hem and finished with an invisible stitch; these were the money-saving methods my mother had taught me growing up. My mother was a mender of both fabric and of men — it wasn't a hobby but a life skill she modeled for me. "We make do," I can hear her say. At the end of the episode, I turned off the TV and handed David his good-as-new pair of pants. Healed, with only a tiny scar of fabric.

Early in the morning, we stood in the foyer of my apartment as David's Uber idled outside in the cul-de-sac. He was on the earliest flight to LA.

"I love you," he said.

"I love you too. Whatever this is, we're going to get through this."

"I know."

"I'll see you in a couple weeks," I reminded him.

"I'll see you in a couple weeks."

We kissed goodbye, and David walked the short distance to the staircase. I stared at the seat of his pants, hoping the patch would hold until he and then I arrived in California. The door to the stairwell closed. He left. An hour later David texted from the runway; he was in tears as his plane was about to take off.

I need you. Please get to me as soon as you can.

I'm coming. I love you, Shew.

I love you too.

Text me when you land.

I will.

Safe flight.

xo, Shew.

I turned off my phone. I went directly to bed and threw the covers over myself. I could smell his cologne, weeks' worth of sex, and I sobbed cradling his pillow until I fell asleep. When I woke up, I opened my laptop and wired two thousand dollars to my immigration lawyer and got to work on our co-created California adventure.

Four weeks later, instead of hopping on a flight and heading west with my worldly possessions, I was in a Toronto hot yoga studio resting in savasana.

I floated above the rubber mat on a layer of sweat. I exhaled. My lungs deflated, and my abdomen relaxed like warm pizza dough on slick beads of olive oil. I inhaled. I felt the distance between my breastbone and the ceiling lessen as my ribs waved like fronds from my spine. With each cycle of breath, I noticed the root of my skull float on the wet nape of my hairline and my pelvis scoop up my groin.

A recorded drone of music bathed the room after an intense hot vinyasa, and a live chant reverberated in my body. Nancy, my teacher, sung the Gayatri mantra, and her rich and bright vocals slid between reciting tones as she soothed our bodies resting in corpse pose. She planted the intention of clarifying our thoughts, our words, and our hearts. "Om, peace peace peace." She sealed the sacred text.

A circle of heat radiated from my chest and my wrists. I felt a shift. When prompted to say namaste, I repeated back the Sanskrit word with feeling, without any sarcasm. I did not, as I had done for years, mentally tag on "Chaka Khan" to diminish its meaning or distance myself from its earnestness. I did not mumble it like I used to when forced to say the Lord's Prayer or amen at family funerals. As I spoke the word, I became aware of my baritone voice. I noticed how much space I occupied instead of how little I was taking up.

After I repeated namaste, I began to weep.

I had made several attempts with yoga and given up. A zealous start always predicted a hard stop. I would enter a studio and snap my mat on the floor, like a beaver thwapping its tail, letting myself be known. My relationship to spaces with mirrored walls and sprung floors is complicated. To enter a studio (or a stage or audition room) was to announce my body and declare its worth. That was my conditioning: to do, to be in service. Making myself useful, contorting my body, or putting on a show — presence-ing myself as an offensive strategy. As if to say to straighter or more masculine, stronger or more perfect bodies, "Don't harm me. I am useful to you."

Yoga teachers would coach me to imagine a candle in the center of the room; to notice that my movements were blowing out the flame. I grew annoyed at being told to breathe, then retold to breathe again. I was prompted into awkward positions but then told not to perform the expression. Finally, I was asked to play dead on the floor. My body did not know how to blend, breathe, not-perform, or relax — especially as a corpse.

Now, lying on the mat I was no longer an enthusiastic twenty-five-year-old aspiring musical theater performer dropping into the splits. I wasn't a thirty-three-year-old solo performer training for stamina. I was a nearly forty-year-old man reckoning with my body in the safety of a room filled with women — not uncommon for me. I was very conscious that I was in a commercial studio full of white bodies dressed in Lululemon speaking one word of half-understood Sanskrit. I questioned my being in this body. Who was I in this moment, on this mat, in this studio? When was the last time I spoke to my body? What age was I? Where did we last leave off?

My body understood the meaning of namaste ("I bow to you") as an invitation to surrender. I was being encouraged not to give up, but to give in. To feel my body relax was both to welcome vulnerability, and to acknowledge that for years I had navigated the world efforting, clenched, and clocking harm.

I was thirty-eight when I finally gave in to gravity.

Resting in savasana with my palms and hips open, I vented an extraordinary amount of heat. My ducts and pores wicked salt, lipids, proteins, minerals, and water, and I started to combust. I melted and became a candle in the center of the room. Whatever secrets hid under layers of fluids and tissue, heat and evaporation would soon be exposed. Perhaps the lost city of Atlantis, a young pharaoh's tomb, the skeletons of treasure hunters: all lay within me.

I surrendered to find out.

Early August 2018

I sat in a small office on the top floor of an unassuming, rather ugly, two-story '70s office building around the corner from my apartment. It's a building I'd walked by every day for over a decade and never even considered that life could survive inside. From the outside, a triptych of windows indicated a hodgepodge of services offered within: a neon sign for palmistry, a dry mount board for accounting, and in between, signless with an aloe vera plant, was Cathie's office.

"The accountant deals with the past, the tarot card reader deals with the future, and I deal with the present," said Cathie, a French-Canadian accent dancing through her words.

Good. She has a sense of humor.

Her curly shoulder-length hair was pulled back in a tight ponytail; she wore a knee-length jean skirt and acid yellow tights with tan suede boots. *We would have eaten lunch together in high school.*

She sat in front of an appealing light moss-green wall; her office was bright, cheerful, not ostentatious. It was a calming container in which to begin a relationship. I looked at the small gray cube clock resting on a glass white coffee table next to her armchair and considered what the next hour would bring. I scanned for the second clock hidden from my eyeline, a water glass, and a tissue box slightly angled towards me: yes, yes, and yes. *The tradecraft is strong.* This was most definitely a therapist's office.

What the fuck are you doing here?

"Shawn, I'm noticing something behind your eyes," she said. "It looks like concern."

I looked out the window and across the street at a yellow building. The midday sun surged and bounced off the light brick color and filled Cathie's office with Renaissance light. I watched the professionals going about their workday, quickly lowering the shades office by office. *The sun is counterproductive to their livelihoods.* I angled myself towards the light so I could comfortably avoid eye contact with Cathie. Birds chirped from a sound machine on the floor by the office door.

"I'm worried that being in therapy might ruin my career," I said.

"How do you mean?" Cathie leaned in.

"I'm worried that I won't be funny anymore."

"I'm sure that won't happen," Cathie reassured. "But so what if you're not funny anymore?"

A high school drama teacher once advised my class to get funny then get serious "like Robin Williams." Mr. Dyke was himself a John Keating character, someone with a genius who didn't fit the constraints of the education system. He was a master of Bouffon clowning and irreverent in his teaching style. He would make us pretend to cry if we corpsed in the middle of an improv scene and laughed at ourselves, at our cleverness. "Cry!" he chastised as he banged on a tambourine. "Cry! Because you are so sad and pathetic!" The cacophony would send everyone in the room into hysterics.

I was genuinely concerned because I had lost my snark, the irreverent tone on which I'd built a career. I was feeling everything instead of dismissing everything as a joke.

"So why are we here today?" Cathie interrupted the silence.

"I think I'm having . . ." I started, then restarted. "I've had mini-breakdowns before, tiny fractures in my sternum, but this is different." I took a shallow breath. "I can't believe I'm saying this."

"Shawn, anything you say here is confidential."

"I think that I am having a spiritual awakening."

I rolled my eyes at my statement, imitating the dismissive swirls friends had made when I confided my experience. The friends who then challenged me to have a nervous breakdown like the rest of the fucking world, or to claim "fatigue" like a celebrity. I was sincere, but it felt foreign and silly to voice. It made me blush with discomfort. I felt clumsy saying it aloud like I was in grade school French class répéter encore une fois a language that was neither part of nor valued in my family. Spirituality was not me. Religion was irrational nonsense: I proudly described myself as an atheist with a Christmas tree. But Cathie did not distance herself from what I was saying. She held space for me.

"I namasted," I said. "Like, in a yoga class, on a mat, with a group of people."

"A lot of people have certain customs or traditions to show reverence."

"Of course," I interrupted. "But I don't. I said namaste, and I meant it." I looked out the window.

"Why did you call the hotline?"

"My stories don't work anymore."

"Say more."

"The stories I used to triage and bandage don't work anymore. It's like I've developed a tolerance to my own narrative."

"That's very good awareness."

"Then my body felt like it was on fire, I started to spin, and so I called."

"I'm glad you picked up the phone."

"I'm thankful you answered."

My chest and wrists had become epicenters of heat, which subsided only when I raised my core temperature in a heated yoga room. I started feeling a burning heat in my body after David began seeing someone new precisely four weeks to the day he issued his ultimatum. He had not been joking about his timeline. In those weeks, I started my immigration process and we continued to be in constant connection while planning a more practical way of being together. Then David, like a stranger, posted a photo to his Instagram: a sexy scruffy-looking queer with curly hair and tattoos after a hike on Angel Island in the middle of the bay. The subject (the person David and I later dubbed the Forest) radiated life. I looked at the photo and immediately knew the context. We can forget the power of a portrait against a landfill of selfies. I knew the look, the glow of the Forest's eyes, because David brought it out in mine.

David insisted that we remain in contact. Where most people (with healthy boundaries) would say no, I said yes. We were both unwilling to let go, and the heat I experienced in my body intensified over the weeks. David's texts and emails and phone calls were charged and confusing, and I was privy to all the details with the Forest. The Forest had the physical relationship I desired, and I dealt with David's erratic emotional needs. David's confessionals aggravated the burn, as if a welding iron slowly circled my ribcage. It hurt, but it was self-inflicted — I could have stopped at any point. I was intentionally leaning into the sizzling pain. The hotter the sensation, the closer I was to finding something lodged inside, embedded like shrapnel. I tunneled into an old wound using David as fuel to propel me deeper.

David's relationship with the Forest made no sense to me. I didn't understand how that shift happened so fast or what I did to cause it. Being flexible while moving in and out of relationships, that plasticity of emotions, wasn't something I could do. Detaching from a boyfriend or friendship always led to inner annihilation — even if I was the one who initiated a breakup. I would drag that ending out and hold on to that final note until the curtain came down and knocked some sense into me. I found friends or gossipy stories of people who just moved on, like a swift change of the wind, fascinating. I observed their new relationships with the confused head tilt of a dog and analyzed them, trying to understand what part of me needed to be fixed or neutered.

At the end of July, David called me crying: he and the Forest were no longer. Meanwhile, I had ripped apart the structures of my life, trying to discover the engine spewing hot exhaust within me. I stopped going to Sunday night dinners with the Bloomfields; I took a break from socializing with Matt; I confronted my father in our first real conversation in twenty years; I distanced myself from friends with terse emails; I cornered my agents into a room and was the exact way you shouldn't be with your representation — honest. I was handing out long overdue fuck-yous left, right, and center. As if I were searching for a necrotic smell, I dismantled everything trying to find a source of rot.

"I went to my doctors. I had my blood tests. So this burning sensation isn't an STI," I informed Cathie.

"That's important to know."

"I keep thinking about that Sufi quote, 'God breaks your heart over and over until it remains open.' I cannot believe I just said that."

"Wow, you have a strong inner critic, don't you?"

No, you don't.

"I do?"

"I would say so."

Don't listen to her.

When I was twelve or thirteen, I was whacked in the face by a line drive softball. I heard two cracks. First, the ball against an aluminum club. Second, the ball against bone. The force knocked me backwards, and I saw stars in broad daylight. The impact spared my front teeth, but blood poured out of my nose like an open faucet. The batter was an adult and a registered nurse. After the second crack, she flung the bat to the side and switched from coach to paramedic. She sat me up, grabbed my nose, and forcefully snapped it back into place. I laughed the entire time. My nose has since been crooked, veering slightly to the right. Heartbreak is like a broken nose. If it's not reset properly, you have to rebreak it over and over — the amount of blood and pain doubles with each reset.

"You have a way with words," Cathie observed after I rounded home plate with my baseball glory.

"It's been my livelihood."

"How exactly?"

"Mining, digesting, transforming all the shit that happens to me for laughs and applause."

My experience as a queer storyteller came with an unfair pressure and expectation that we only get to tell our stories once. The telling must be perfectly crafted, accessible, and entertaining, and in that demand, a pattern develops. The processing of traumatic events, digested and repeated in a version fit for consumption, reinforced a history that was disconnected from my actual experience. I became the stories that were more tolerable for others to hear.

"Shawn, when you say this, my arms fall off."

Confused by her statement, I looked at Cathie's arms, which remained completely attached at her shoulders. "Not sure I follow."

Cathie shrugged her shoulders to her ears then mimed the left then the right arm falling off and smashing on the ground. It felt like watching a Second City student trying to establish an action while their scene partner freezes in confusion.

"I still don't get it," I admitted.

She resettled her body and pivoted her approach. "I would like to hear your story."

There on a gray IKEA couch, I performed an abridged sit-down version of my life story. Just casually offering the highs and lows to a stranger, writing off complex relationships, glazing over developmental trauma, and breaking the tension with some of my best jokes. Cathie sat stoically rooted in her occasional chair. *Tough audience.*

"Shawn, when you tell me this, I feel angry for you," Cathie said.

The word *anger* felt dangerous. The anger I knew was unpredictable, physical — the violence and rage I'd experienced in my childhood. It felt like something I wasn't entitled to express. *Nobody likes an angry gay man.*

"You told me this story like it's a routine. What if this isn't funny? What if what happened to you as a child was wrong?"

Cathie wasn't a tough audience; she was the first professional empath I'd met. Which was terrifying. I broke my eye contact with her and looked out the window, but I could no longer focus on office workers, their menial tasks, or the details of the building. My sight was blurry, my eyes plump with tears.

"Why are you sad?"

"Because no one has ever said that it was wrong what happened to me." My voice cracked.

My family and I were related by blood, but we weren't attached by the same story. Many of my relatives were livid at me for writing a memoir, not because the stories were untrue, but because I'd spoken them. Rosie O'Donnell once said that in a family of dysfunction, you are not allowed to address what is directly in front of you.

A few tears escaped from my eyes, and I did my best to suck them back in.

"Why did you stop yourself from crying?"

That is just what you do.

"That is just what you do!"

"What are you feeling?" asked Cathie. "What were those tears?" She baited her question on a shiny hook and it sunk down inside my body, where it plunked into an abyss.

I thought about the ingredients that made that particular tear. *Don't think about that.*

I looked at Cathie.

"I feel like my entire life I've been screaming, 'Where are the adults?' and I realize that I'm a thirty-eight-year-old divorced, heartbroken comedian still waiting for the adults to show up. But the adults never show up."

"How do you know this?"

"Because I'm the adult, and I'm not present. I'm not here."

I could hear David's voice echoing in my statement. My shoes dug into the sand of Ocean Beach, and my chest roared with heat.

"How does this make you feel?"

"Angry."

Anger was the source of my discomfort. The long burn overwhelming my body caused an abrupt thaw and molecules of anger, no longer frozen, pressurized inside me to dangerously high levels.

I was angry. I walked on scorched earth and with each step there was a moan, an ache. I imagined this stirring as what environmental scientists and climate experts must feel when they witness entire species wiped from existence or when ice caps calve and dissolve into the ocean. They can shout their knowing for all to hear, but they can't stop the progression. My anger was waking up to plastic straws lodged in sea turtles and exhausted polar bears swimming. My anger was navigating life beyond the tipping point, witnessing the unstoppable fallout, and knowing this was nature's way of starting over. Anger was like a clear-cut forest, and Cathie was inviting me to step on a stump and connect with the severed roots underfoot, to reconnect with an ecology that had existed before being sawed apart. The valve snapped off, a flood of tears erupted from my eyes. Cathie watched as I emptied myself with an unstoppable downpour.

Cry! Cry because you are so sad and pathetic!

"Shawn, who shows up for you?" she asked once the tears had abated.

"What?" I stumbled. The question echoed David.

"Who shows up for you?" she repeated.

"I show up for me."

"Okay. Who else?"

"Matt. Matt shows up for me."

"Good," Cathie said. "Matt shows up for you. Let's start there."

Cathie and I ended our first session by committing to doing the heavy lifting of reconnecting my anger. *And you thought you wanted to be happy.*

I soon learned therapy is not like spring cleaning a closet; it is not a process of quickly sorting and pitching everything over the course of a rainy afternoon. Things sprawl over the floor for months at a time. It is a week-by-week process of deciding what to keep, what to discard, what to repair, what has value, what once worked but no longer does. It's about sitting with chaos and allowing things to be unsightly. Therapy, for me, was about ripping off the hinges to the closet door and exposing the mess.

We started deconstructing my stories, dividing the performative pieces from the folklore of my body. Humans are a species of storytellers; we make meaning and craft narratives with intent. We skip over pages, redact to avoid embarrassment, and add white space for poetry. We shave off the details and round the edges as we become our story. But the body isn't a clever writer: it's an archivist that accounts for everything, and like invisible ink, secrets in my body would reveal themselves with intense heat.

Cathie would be my guide and companion as an unknown storm approached, the Samwise to my Frodo. She would seek resources for herself to support me in what life was about to offer. She would weep, laugh at the absurdity, sit in the discomfort, and grieve the men I loved. I would pass her the box of tissues and check in to see if she, too, was okay, because we were in a dance of death together. I can say I am alive, without exaggeration or hyperbole, because of her — because of accessible, affordable mental healthcare.

Through all that was to follow, she would root me with one question, prompting me to listen from the bottom up.

"Can you feel your feet?"

SKIN

September 17, 2018

Rebel House was our local, and Matt and I were creatures of habit. The cramped cottage-chic tavern in stuffy and elitist Rosedale was subversive amidst upscale restaurants and boutiques. During our relationship, Matt and I marched downhill weekly for the generous basket of kettle fries. We were like William Lyon Mackenzie, who led a rebellion down Yonge Street in 1837 against loyalist forces (and lost). The wood tables are inlayed with the shape of a hanged man, a grim commemoration of the rebels executed by the loyalists. The pub was my territory after our breakup, but that boundary was now a détente.

Three summers had passed, and Matt and I sat outside enjoying one of the last beautiful nights before the insurgence of fall. A giant red and white parachute hoisted on a king pole transformed the back courtyard into a circus tent, shading guests from the sun during the day, trapping warmth from the heat lamps at night.

Mature red hot peppers grew up the high fences, and Toronto's infamous racoons scaled down the walls. They scurried underneath the benches of unfazed urbanites as their paws scratched at the interlocking brick. The patio is a secret, a place you'd know only as a local; you don't read about it on a top ten of the city list. Matt had arrived straight from work, the first couple buttons of his collared shirt undone to expose the scoop line of a white tank top, tufts of chest hair poking out on his tanned skin. This look was a new side of Matt who for years buttoned his shirts right to the collar, hiding his broad chest; now he had matured into his shape. He sat sideways on his chair, extending his long legs, crossing them at his shins. His pants were rolled up, as they always were, to reveal his ankles.

We were celebrating Matt's birthday, the highest of holidays, an occasion more important than Christmas. Every year it was the one day (stretched over seven) when Matt celebrated the miracle of his birth with the swagger of a Supreme Leader of a totalitarian state: events marked with photoshoots, house parties, custom T-shirts, dinners, a carrot cake or three. He indulged in celebrating himself as his annual excuse to step into the footlights (where he belonged) while treading the delicate balance between narcissism and joy. He glowed naturally, but even more so on his birthday.

Two wheat beers arrived at our table in the hands of Guy, the snarky but kind bartender. He placed my pint down first. I passed the glass to Matt as the second beer was placed front of me.

"Nice to see you gays back together. You need more time before ordering?"

"We do. I think we're going to be here till close. We're celebrating Matt's birthday."

"Well, happy birthday. I'm not fucking singing."

I never missed or forgot Matt's birthday. But I never remembered his birthdate or telephone number, and this made him percolate with anger. This fact was the first thing he brought up in couples therapy. He started drilling me like a math tutor, over and over to no avail. I knew emotionally when his birthday was (he was a cuspy Leo), but my brain cannot retain numbers. I've only ever remembered four sequences of numbers: my social insurance number, my telephone number, my parents' telephone number, and my Ontario health card number. I can remember the garnishes on a hamburger I ate in 1987 and what song was on the radio while I chewed, but multiply eight by seven? *It's fifty-something-ish.* This year, Matt's thirty-second, I bowed out of the traditional birthday celebration with the city family for the first time. Louisa and I hadn't spoken since early July, and I'd offered my seat for a lavish dinner at a trendy restaurant to Matt's new boyfriend. Tonight was a private belated celebration.

"This is on me."

"Shawn, you don't have to." Matt smiled with the promise of a free meal.

"Yes. Yes I do," I countered. "I skipped your dinner. Plus you saved me in the park."

～～

"It's okay, Shawn. Breathe." Matt put his giant arms around me and pulled me into his chest. "Breathe."

It was a humid July night, and Matt and I were in a moonlit park working through the last six months of my life. I was experiencing the second wave of my first-ever panic attack.

A few hours before Sunday night dinner, David had posted that first photo of the Forest. The image sliced through my chest. My heart fell, smashed against my stomach, then shattered in the bowl of my pelvis, and scraping against bone, it sparked. A flame smoldered in the trunk of my body, like a knob and tube fire in the walls of an old home. The flashpoint caught decayed horsehair and newsprint before burning up the wood lath. Silent, smokeless, it went unnoticed as it incinerated support beams until the entire house collapsed without warning. Messages back and forth between iPhones did nothing to snuff the embers. David had posted the photo with intention, and he admitted he did not care about how I felt. We were over. *You are disposable.*

When I arrived at dinner I was unknowingly engulfed. We had gathered at a favorite Italian restaurant, a local chain that was more of a cafeteria for the wealthy who really, really, really appreciate white marble finishings. I should have canceled last minute, made a simple excuse like a headache, but my own insistence on trudging through difficult circumstances meant I pulled my chair up to the table burning hotter than the oven cranking out twenty-five-dollar dried-out thin-crust pizzas. Matt, Daccia, and Louisa were well pressed and had their best social faces on. I widened my eyes at Daccia — our sibling-like shorthand — and she confirmed message received by tucking a long curl of thick chestnut hair behind her ear. She smiled and took a deep breath. Knowing I would struggle through this dinner, she took the reins of the conversation.

Daccia lifted her wine glass, her bracelets clanking together. "Well cheers, everyone."

"Cheers! Salut!"

The dynamic of our supper club had shifted after George died. There was a jarring reconfiguration to the roles we played after the stately presence who once sat at the head of the table and picked up the check was gone. Matt and Louisa fused their own special relationship, and Daccia and I joked that Matt was the favorite because he was always served the first and largest slice of dessert. I felt a growing existential exhaustion in my life, and more and more I struggled with my ability to feign being okay or happy. I questioned if I could offer anything of value or interest to the weekly conversations. I wondered how often Daccia regretted bringing me home to meet her parents nearly two decades ago. I found myself emotionally eating (in the company of others) and drinking myself to the point of mansplaining. I had buffered my relationship to these tablemates with language that created an arm's-length distance — peppering diminishing words like *faux*, *fake*, *city*, *ex*, *common law*, *in-law* before titles like *family*, *mother*, *father*, *sister*, and *husband*. That dismissive distance was a source of anguish with a sense of protection. *Is this real?* I thought. *Or are we just pretending?*

"Why is it so fucking hot in this restaurant?" I hadn't meant to say that out loud.

I could not pretend. I was thirsty, guzzling water, sweating through my collared shirt, and unfocused. Twice I excused myself to the washroom to read David's angry texts. He had flipped the situation so that somehow I was in the wrong for ruining the moment of his joyful photo. On the second trip I read, "I want a Matt deal." I was split in two: I was at dinner with my family, with my ex-husband, and on a virtual oceanside beach arguing with David. I could no longer be split between my physical and digital worlds.

Life has handed me enough trials. I'd like to think that I am made of diamonds or impervious to challenges, but a fissure erupted in my sternum and I cracked in the bathroom stall of a Terroni. The collapse of my worlds, my first panic attack ever was set to the ambient sounds of an Italian language recording: "*Grazie* means thank you. Grazie . . . thank you. Grazie . . . thank you. *Prego* means you're welcome. Prego . . . you're welcome. Prego . . . you're welcome. When saying thank you very much, just add *tante*. Grazie tante . . . thank you very much. Grazie tante . . ." I collected myself, splashed my face with water, returned to the table, and then ate a half-melted affogato.

As we said our goodbyes outside the restaurant, I whispered to Matt that I needed to talk; I sensed a countdown before my second Italian gratitude lesson. We walked to a nearby park, and my entire being unfurled in front of him. There are not many humans who would walk an ex through a second heartbreak, nor would they go to an Adele concert, celebrate holidays, run towards each other in the street, exchange house keys, share Netflix accounts, or plan trips. Not many would cheer on their ex while they wrote about their relationship, nor would they be the first in line to buy the book. Not many would fill in as bartender at an event or offer last-minute stage directions before a curtain. But that was Matt. That was us. We had history.

"He said he wants a Matt deal."

"Fuck that! A Matt deal? There is only one Matt deal in your life."

"I know there is only one Shawn in yours."

"Does he even know how much work that was? You and me?"

"I know."

"Fuck him!" Matt exploded. "A fucking Matt deal? The nerve."

"He asked me to marry him."

"What!?"

"I said yes," I admitted in embarrassment.

"You said yes? To marriage? With him?" His voice cracked with hurt. "You said . . ."

Matt puffed himself up like a wrestler entering a ring, waving his arms and pounding his chest to the delight of the trees. "No! No! No!"

Matt never lost his temper; he was even-keeled and didn't let the weight of the world affect him. He was naturally soft-spoken, his voice purred, and he passively leaned back in his worldly interactions, so watching him act out forcefully and aggressively revealed a new balance in our relationship. He was guarding me with an uncharacteristically dominant display by flapping his limbs and wagging his finger, whooshing away the nonsense of this gay drama. For years, I had been the caretaker to any upset that came Matt's way. He used my "attack dog," the unattractive part of my personality that was pure scrappy self-defense, to offload any task that would upset his laissez-faire sunny disposition. I was not only his fixer and his enforcer but also his writer of terse emails and his human resource lawyer. David was encroaching on Matt's territory with a sense of entitlement, and this flared a rage in Matt that was delightful to witness. There was something vital he felt he needed to protect. *Who is this?*

Matt placed his paper napkin on his lap, then positioned his side plate in anticipation of the food we'd just ordered.

"So, I'm seeing a therapist," I said.

"Good. How's that?"

"I'm going once a week." I laughed. "Yoga is also helping."

"See! I told you you needed to practice yoga."

"I've stolen your sangha."

"It's yours."

I didn't have to work, sitting with Matt. I missed this ease, and sadness bubbled up. I let tears roll down my face. It was a new vulnerability I was showing him, the side of me that admitted I wasn't in control. Matt reached over the divide marked by salt and pepper shakers and placed his palm on my right hand. His large meaty hand covered mine with his summer olive skin. I remembered the time we sat in the back of the pub and overhead a couple in their early sixties break up in the corner booth. The blindsided woman reacted with tears and blame; the stoic man sat in silence after asking for a divorce. Matt and I had locked stares, our eyes widened, savoring the deliciousness of the conversation. Now, with tears flowing down my face, I sensed the table next to us grow quiet and still.

"It's like for years my arms were flailing around and I didn't notice. Everywhere I went I was failing, and I didn't have any awareness. It was destructive, and I'm really angry."

"It's okay."

"I know. This is who I am now. The guy who cries through a spiritual awakening."

"Oh no. Don't tell me you drank the Jesus juice?" Matt laughed.

"Spirituality is different than theology."

"I know," he interrupted. "I watched that episode of *Oprah* too."

"I'm saying *awakening*. Because it doesn't feel like a break-*down* but break*through*."

Two more pints arrived with the appetizers: a feast of pâté and crostini, wings, kettle fries, and a side of pickled beets. Matt's petal-shaped eyes bloomed twice their size, and his head bobbled back and forth as he wiggled his fingers like tentacles towards the kettle fries. Matt could eat until he was sick and moaning on the ground, but he ate with appreciation and joy. *Abbondanza.*

The dining table was the altar of our relationship, and we continued to nourish it by eating together. Staying connected was a choice, and we shifted our relationship in ways that others failed: a result of time, communication, and clear boundaries. But it wasn't without hurt.

In the whole of our relationship, Matt and I fought twice. First, an argument over an unpaid hydro bill just before we split up. *It wasn't about your hydro bill.* Second, a real confrontation, shortly after our decision to part, while we were still living together. Matt stumbled home at dawn from partying with his new volleyball friends. *A gay sports league is the death of any long-term relationship.* We continued to share a bed, and I had gone sleepless without a call or text. I took all of his belongings and placed them at the front door so that when Matt entered the apartment, he faced a pivotal choice: he could gather his things, the cat, and leave immediately, or stay and treat our relationship with the care it deserved. If Matt stayed, he would commit to eating dinner every Sunday with the Bloomfields and in return I would carry the blame for the failure of our relationship when the topic came up. I offered him a *Gilmore Girls* deal. Matt was drunker than I had ever seen him, and his voice was hoarse from talking; the more he drank the louder he got. It was unfair to blindside him, but I was fighting for the integrity of a relationship. It was the absolute first time I'd confronted him with my attack dog, which he'd only ever enjoyed protection from. That morning, I left the apartment to purchase a new mattress at the Hudson's Bay, and when I returned Matt was sleeping in our bed. All of his things were back in their place. We slept side by side for another month.

"Your face when I walked through that door." Matt laughed. "I'd never seen you so angry."

"It was worth it."

"I could make you do anything, even if you didn't want to," he admitted for the first time while pulling at the last bit of chicken stuck in the wing flat with his perfect teeth.

"Remember when I washed out your moving van before you left?"

"Yep." He smiled.

Two grilled cheeses with peameal bacon served half fries and half salad with a pickle arrived on the table, and Guy followed in with another round of pints. Matt took the ketchup bottle and squeezed a puddle for dipping.

"Do you think you'll start coming back to dinner?" Matt asked.

As I weeded through my life, Sunday night dinners had ended up on the chopping block. The family dynamic needed to shift to allow for an alternate ending. The fantasy that Matt and I would reunite and wed was dead. For a year, I had carried around that hope. I fixed everything: I got out of debt, I had a savings account, I lost weight, and I did whatever I could think of to be a better partner. I had waited for Matt — as did most of our community — but it didn't happen. I needed to move forward. Unfortunately, when your entire nervous system is a nuclear reactor without water, there is no way to request time and space politely. You blow up, and people start running. Family is family — faux, city, chosen, or blood.

"I have to repair things with Louisa. I did a lot of damage."

"You still moving to California?"

"I'm moving to California," I said. "Going down mid-November to scout neighborhoods."

"Are you moving for David?"

Don't say for David.

"I'm moving because it feels like the right career move."

You two can't hide from each other.

"I don't like him. He's not right for you."

It felt unfair for Matt to say this. It reminded me of when he'd told me he didn't like the shade of gray I painted the living room after he left.

"I know you don't like him. But what if this is about me and my what's next? We both know I waited long and hard for you to come back."

"True."

We sat awkwardly in silence as sadness flooded our eyes. We always said that we would grow old together, we just didn't know how or what that would look like.

Matt's chin was angled slightly down as he picked at the bits of fried potatoes left sprinkled on his plate. His brown hair was thinning ever so slightly on top of his head, his arms were strong, his body was toned and full. It filled me with joy to see him age with such beauty. There were moments where I didn't recognize this man who was once my partner, and I wondered if I met him now what sort of life we'd create together and how it would differ from the relationship that led to our oneness and codependency.

Our separation was a process of relearning how to swim by ourselves and we thrived and grew from it. We generated a new lung and learned how to breathe from the depths of that new lobe. An arm formed from the stump of our once-conjoined shoulders and learned to tread water. Our thighs could hold space next to each other without needing to touch.

The afternoon Matt and I decided that our partnership was indeed over, we fell mewling into each other. The truth formed into an ominous figure in the room. We were scared and wounded animals. "I'm sorry. I love you. I'm sorry. I love you. I'm sorry. I love you," we repeated as our cells began to separate. We kissed between words to ease the ripping sensation as truth unzipped us from head to toe. It seared like a Band-Aid slowly being removed, tugging at every follicle and flake of skin: the wide strip of adhesive ran the lengths of our bodies. Truth was cruel and methodical, like a cousin twisting the flesh of your forearm in opposite motions with a snake bite. After we had purged our sadness, Matt was first to stand. He held out his hand, lifted me off the floor, and led us to our bed. We slept side by side, practicing separation through incremental distances: the minute discomfort of a nanometer, millimeter, centimeter to the destabilizing realness of a foot, meter, mile. Matt and I stood face-to-face and uncoupled by taking one baby step back from each other, then another. At each new separation we nurtured the strength of our evolving connection. It took summers to test beyond the width of a dinner table. Seasons had now passed but the concept of living on opposite coasts in different countries was still unimaginably painful.

"California is far."

"It's only a five-hour flight."

"I don't know life without you."

"I don't either."

We sat in silence.

"We're always connected no matter where I am," I said. "Besides, you have this handsome, kind, young boyfriend to concern your future with."

Matt grinned.

An apple crumble arrived in front of Matt with no song — as promised. I lifted my near-empty pint glass and made a toast to a bright year ahead and to the unknown. We sealed the wish by dipping our spoons into the mixture of warm fruit, sugary oats, and cold vanilla ice cream. It wasn't carrot cake, but it was delicious.

People throw around the word *soulmate* casually, reducing it to an elevated best friend forever. But to me, soulmate defies nomenclature. To commit to a soulmate means to acknowledge that love is non-binary, for the spirit to state bravely that relational contracts are not static agreements but sacred and shapeshifting entities. Force it into a form that is too small, and it will suffocate and atrophy. The flexibility of our love was put under immense pressure; we watched it morph, accepted its new shape. Matt and I tested as soulmates. We had done our work and embraced our new state. Our relationship had a capacity greater than we could have ever imagined: we were truly separate but together.

I paid the bill on our way out. I walked Matt to his bike before starting to say goodbye. As he unlocked his bike, I looked at Matt's feet and smiled. He wore vintage dock shoes with a hard heel and no socks. He begrudgingly wore boots in the winter, he wore running shoes for exercise, but any other time he only wore Top-Siders. He'd worn them as a kid, and now as an adult had a permanent tan line that ringed from his heel deep along his metatarsals; his heel had a notched callous from where the leather topline of the backstay clicked into his skin. Matt would wear a pair of shoes until the soles split or his toe popped out; even then he would purchase a tube of glue before splurging and breaking in a new pair. He like things old and worn in. These shoes were almost ten years old.

"Matt, do you think you should be riding in those shoes? Your foot could slip off the pedal! How do you even get traction?" I caught myself: my old relational habit was popping up.

Matt laughed.

"If I say 'ride safe,' is that still mothering?"

"No. But yes, Shawn. I will ride safe."

We embraced.

"This was wonderful," I said.

"It was. I'm full and a bit drunk."

"Perfect. Happy birthday."

"Thank you."

We kissed, a connection that went beyond lust, need, or want. Matt put on his bike helmet, and my anxiety relaxed.

"I love you, Elby. I always will," I said.

"I love you, too, Bert."

I watched Matt's red bicycle light blink off into the night. I stood waving until he pedaled out of my sight. I took a deep breath. The autumnal night air rolled in, crisp in the lungs and sobering with each exhale. I turned on my heels and prepared myself for the steady incline up Yonge Street. My heart was full, even more than my stomach. I felt unconditionally loved.

The swings of my childhood were bone-breaking, tetanus-laden tests of fate. Warped planks bound to decommissioned hydro poles with rusted chains; discs of plywood threaded with a knot only slightly bigger than the center hole; spindly branches of a willow tree gathered, clutched in a fist, and held onto for dear life. There were no safety stops or rubber crash pads.

The objective was to gain enough momentum to launch yourself into the air, to defy gravity for a split second, to hover weightlessly. Then fall, ever so slightly, and feel the jerk of a taut rope catch your body weight and hoist your stomach into your throat. Of course, there were the daredevils; the fearless farm kids who jumped mid-air and flew like Superman and broke their arms like Clark Kent.

I was a fan of Batman. Batman drank Diet Coke.

All summer long we encouraged each other to "go higher, higher," fully aware the rotted seat could crack in two and send us plummeting to the hard earth below. "Don't stop!" Our flapping T-shirts and the skin on our faces measured velocity; our feet dug trenches in the sand grain by grain. "Higher! Higher!" we called, despite the fact that the closest adult was fields away drinking Seagram's coolers and Labatt Blue.

My grandpa Clarence hung a tire swing off an old black walnut tree by the corral where he fed his cattle in the warm months. My sister, cousins, and I used to rock on the worn-out wheel while watching him call in the cows. Climbing onto the tire was a rodeo challenge — the prickly yellow rope blistered our hands red, the tire treads collapsed and pinched the backs of our thighs. The u-shaped bottom of the tire collected rain and splashed our legs with warm brown water boiled by the sun. It was a rubber-and-rope Gravitron, but without the flashing lights, heavy metal music, or smoking carnies. We spun for hours, dizzying ourselves, the farmland a smear of green, yellow, blue. We'd fall off onto the ground laughing, trying not to vomit up the tumblers of cherry Kool-Aid and cans of orange C'plus in our bellies. We'd roll on the grass, covered in pungent split walnut seeds shaped like pig snouts, and we'd hold them to our faces. We'd snort, mimicking the pink creatures rolling in the mud on the other side of the fence.

"When pigs fly," the animals oinked back in laughter.

It was early morning when my cousin Heather and I sneaked outside to practice our circus flips off the A-frame of her blue swing set. We were beginner trapeze artists who spent one summer in the late '80s teaching ourselves death-defying gymnastics. We graduated from seated swings to swinging while standing, from balancing on one foot to hanging by both arms off the top bar. Within weeks we were able to swing, stand, pull up, flip over, and nail a landing in one fluid motion.

The morning dew had not evaporated before my first attempt on the top bar. My hand slipped as my chest cleared the rung. As I fell, my torso caught the rusted ridges of an eye bolt and my skin tore from my navel to chin. I landed with a thud. My aunt and uncle woke up to the sounds of me sobbing and bleeding as Heather led me into their bedroom. My uncle calmly reached for a tin of ointment in his bedside table. He began slathering a thick wave of goo over the torn flesh, using his fingernails to graft parts of my skin back in place. I can't picture my uncle's face then, but I remember his enormous calloused hands sealing my wound. The back and forth sensation of a thick index finger cauterizing the bleeding under grease. His touch coagulated my tears.

What practice I had as a child moving from extreme to extreme. In conversation with my emotions, with my body; with gravity, friction, tension; with the physical world. Gliding, back and forth through time, between the past and the present. From sheer terror to happiness, up and down, unconsciously asking, "Where is my body in relationship to the earth? Am I going forward or backwards? Who will catch me if I fall?" Unwittingly I prepared for the disorienting moments ahead. For that day when the branch breaks, the rope snaps, the seat cracks, and it all comes crashing down to the earth.

October 29, 2018

"It's time!" Elaine Stritch shouts at the end of her iconic one-woman-show At Liberty. *"It's time!" The Broadway legend imitates a child actor joyfully running by dressing rooms, rousing the seasoned actors before curtain call. "It's time!" Matt and I listen to the recording with full hearts as we cross the Quebec border into Ontario. Essential listening on our rainy drive home from Quispamsis, New Brunswick, several years ago.*

"Gentlemen," interrupted the doctor, "it's time."

The chief doctor — tall, burly, Scottish — stood at the foot of two lines of us flanking the hallway outside a private waiting room in the hospital's burn unit. I reluctantly held the hand of Matt's dad, joining the Friends, the Boyfriend, and the Stepmom as they prayed. I wasn't yet comfortable facing my spiritual beliefs on my own, let alone in a group. A last-minute adoption of faith in life's darkest moments felt like unpreparedness rather than comfort. I dropped Matt's father's hand like an impatient child. Holding hands as a group felt like a privilege, skin touching skin in a unit with regimented protocols to preserve, repair, and regrow the body's casing.

It was a rainy Monday just before five o'clock. The nightmare began for me early Sunday morning when I woke up to a phone screen littered with missed calls and unread messages. I drew my worst forgone conclusion, and a return call prompted in me only short shock statements.

"Fire? Matt? Cat? Fire? The fucking candles!" I roared, waking the entire cul-de-sac. "Fuck!"

I called Louisa.

The news ripped throughout our community in the fifteen-minute car ride between my apartment and Sunnybrook Hospital. My jovial Uber driver asked several times about my morning while I stared blankly out the window. "Great! Just going to see my aunt at the hospital," I lied. *Your aunt?*

I texted David, still asleep in Los Angeles: "En route to the hospital. Matt had an accident. His Halloween costume caught fire. I have to help take him off life support. Please call when you wake up."

My phone erupted with condolences barely masking curiosity. "Thank you, but he's still alive," I replied. Texts became my sole transmissions from the abyss, the only way to say the unimaginable and unthinkable, a tether as my experience crawled to a halt and the outside world sped onward. The car pulled in front of the hospital main entrance and my driver begged for a five-star rating.

I entered the private waiting room. A team of five doctors stopped their briefing and the room went silent. *Game over.* I saw the shocked and shrunken Friends who'd witnessed the accident. The Boyfriend and his family.

"Hey kids," I found myself saying. *Hey kids?*

For the first time in two years, I saw Matt's dad, who had taken the first flight in from Saint John. He stood and hugged me. "Thank you for coming."

Very early in our relationship, Matt chased me around the apartment with his phone, screaming, "My father wants to talk to you!" Matt wrestled me on our bed and pinned the phone to my ear. "I hear you drink gin and tonic," said the Dad. His voice exactly matched Matt's hilarious impersonation. Matt had felt comfortable enough in our relationship not necessarily to "come out" but to implicitly confirm his sexuality with his family. But I was oblivious to this then. In the way his family accepted him, with the ease and openness they welcomed me into their family, I just assumed it was long-held knowledge. That summer, Matt and I first drove out to the East Coast, our journey underscored by recordings of Broadway divas, for me to meet his family and extended family. In the driveway of his home, the Dad extended his hand and said in his chugging East Coast accent, "I'm not going to hug you, but I'll shake your hand." Matt burst into laughter.

I grew to regard the Dad as family, a father-in-common-law.

A Friend vacated a seat so that I was front and center to the conversation.

I was an adult in the room.

My iPhone vibrated incessantly.

It was time. The prayer formation broke apart and the Boyfriend and I were shuttled towards a dressing station. Two nurses suited us up in gowns. Me wearing yellow would be Matt's last laugh. He ruthlessly skewered any redhead he saw wearing the color. Matt had a ribbon of cattiness woven into the airy chiffon of his personality. He was also mischievous, a trickster, and a spring-time jerk who found pleasure in crushing the hollow heads of milk chocolate Easter bunnies. For Lent, we stopped going into the drugstore because he would be killing rabbits like Glenn Close in *Fatal Attraction*. Once at Sunday dinner, we completed the *New York Times*'s psychopath test, and Matt scored very (very) high. It was a surprise side of him that he only shared with his intimate connections. It was delightful.

The nurses tucked the sleeves of the gowns into the thick bands of latex gloves. We were spared wearing masks and were offered mints to freshen our breath. The protective gear made the nurses and doctors hard to identify, a medical masquerade. I can't remember their names, but I knew them by their care. I remember the kindness in their eyes, a curl along their hairline, the way they lent us their strength. Blue Eyeliner, the unit's trauma counselor, came out of her office and took over for a nurse tying up the back of my gown. She then placed her hands on my shoulders to ground me. She saw me.

~ ~

"I know who you are." Blue Eyeliner assessed me as she leaned against the edge of her cluttered desk. She'd plucked me from the hallway with a you-me-my-office-now gesture just minutes after the Dad and I had decided to remove Matt's life support.

"And who is that?" I sank into a worn armchair.

"You're the First Wife."

Decoding heteronormative comparisons is exhausting, but there was a blunt, no-bullshit quality to her knowing that I immediately appreciated and connected with. She'd introduced herself to everyone in the private waiting room by simply stating, "This is shit." Her clarity, her exactness in language placed us all on the same level, understanding that there was no use in making meaning from a senseless accident. It was shit, and this was not the time to be coddled with clichés, to attempt to bypass the pain. The sentiments that popped up on my iPhone — all love, light, and reincarnation — skipped over the process of death, the reality in front of us. Platitudes are dangerously lazy, especially when used to erase a most significant moment in a person's life. What this moment called for was to walk directly through the pain and discomfort, to be sober and present, and to feel every second.

"Do I get to choose if I'm Bette, Diane, or Goldie?"

Blue Eyeliner laughed.

"We all see you. Everyone on this floor knows exactly who you are. We all think you're handling this with grace."

Grace. The word felt alien, not associated with me.

"Why does it feel like I'm about to lose both my husband and my child?" I disintegrated into tears.

"Perhaps it's time to stop mothering men."

"No shit," I lobbed back.

"Do you feel like you raised him?"

"We raised each other."

"How so?"

"We were kids. Matt wasn't even out to his family. We didn't have support or money, but we created a huge life from nothing but ourselves. You don't see my family in that room, do you? Matt is my everything, and I'm losing that."

"Would you like a drink?" She pointed to her desk drawer.

"No thanks."

"You sure? 'Cause the next few months are going to be rough."

A gentle warning offered from someone masterfully trained in quickly assessing personality types and behavioral patterns. Blue Eyeliner was like a telescope seeing far in the distance, but her feet along with her professional care were grounded in the hospital.

I made a mental note to buy a bottle of bourbon.

Blue Eyeliner walked the Boyfriend and me, the First Wife, towards Matt. He was in a south-facing private room with an unobstructed view of the Don Valley through panoramic windows. The late autumn leaves finally had turned with the approach of November, although four days of constant drizzle and gray had dulled the majesty. Every doctor and nurse of D7 was present, forming a semicircle outside the room by the nursing station to receive us. A separate team of doctors sat to the right behind gray monitors. I have been walked several times to an awaiting crew on set, producers and assistants huddled behind monitors, but this wasn't a medical drama. This was reality in the form of a nightmare. I had an astronaut's anxiety, as if I were marching towards a rocket to be blasted into a new realm.

I saw Curly Hair, the nurse who had first led me in to the room yesterday morning. Matt had been lying sedated, covered in thick layers of gauze, hooked to a multi-drum machine churning and pumping various drugs and sedatives into his body. The device looked like a medical grade Slurpee machine from 7-Eleven. Slushies were Matt's Kryptonite: three sips and he would collapse holding his stomach from the concentrated syrup. Forty units of fluid flushing through Matt's system made him unrecognizable, but I knew him by his wide nostrils, short torso, long legs, and large feet.

I walked out of the room. "I can't fix this," I declared to Curly Hair.

"Oh, no honey." She squeezed my upper arms while stripping me of my gear. "I'm sorry, but you can't, nor are you expected to."

Curly Hair then walked me to a nearby private washroom and lowered me to the ground and closed the door as she left. My face pressed against the cold bathroom floor. I felt relief knowing that Matt wasn't in pain. I was certain of this because he wasn't rolling his ankles. Matt rolled his ankles in discomfort when he was sick with a flu or cold. It's how I knew when it was time to drag him to a walk-in clinic. *He feared going to the doctor.* I lay on the floor watching my phone buzz with messages. After I recovered, I picked myself off the floor then started practicing going in and out of Matt's room, taking longer each time, building a tolerance to being there. Eventually I was able to sit with Matt and listen to an audiobook, though the medical staff didn't know whether or not Matt would understand or hear it.

Now, the Boyfriend and I sat in silence at Matt's bedside. The chief doctor entered the room with the calm and confidence of an orchestra conductor. "Gentlemen, we will now begin the end of life ritual," said the Doctor.

Ritual? The word conjured pop-culture images of sacrifice, the occult. But this end of life ritual was neutral, a step-by-step procedure to humanely ease the transition of the dying with the support of medical knowing — a slow shift from machine to mortal, a bridge that allows nature to resume its due course without suffering.

The digital clock on the wall at the left of Matt's bed read five-zero-zero.

"If you could look away," instructed the Doctor. "We will now remove the breathing tube."

The Boyfriend and I looked away. I heard a hollow clicking sound, and my eyes focused on the floor. To the left of my shoes by the wheel of the bed was a smear of Matt's dried blood. It looked painted on the linoleum. I wanted to reach down with a tissue, wet with the salt of my tears, and preserve a relic. Instead, I clasped the Boyfriend's hand and squeezed.

Matt and I both had agreed: our time was our time. "Just like Donna," we'd remind each other. Donna Sherman was a prominent voice teacher at the Royal Conservatory of Music and a longtime friend of the Bloomfields. Donna was getting takeout at King's Noodle on Spadina, while we were there observing our Sunday night dinner. Louisa invited her to join us at our table, and Donna declined by holding up two large containers filled with soup and sing-saying, "No thanks! I'm having broth." She glowed with a fey disposition. "I'm dyyyy-ing!" Donna laughed from the pit of her being, turned on her heels, and hummed herself out of the restaurant. Matt and I both keeled over in laughter. Donna passed just weeks later.

Angel Eyes, the attending nurse, asked if she could sit in the room during Matt's transition, and I welcomed the additional company. The Boyfriend pressed play on his iPhone and slid it into a red Solo cup. In the hours before the ritual, I asked for a playlist of Matt's favorite songs to be created. It was a simple flip of mindset, away from last-minute miracles and divine intervention towards the reality that if we cannot grant him life, then we must grant him a peaceful goodbye. "Beautiful" by Christina Aguilera filled the room.

"Elby," I say softly. "We're right here beside you. Outside this room are the kindest doctors and nurses. Your parents and your friends. We're all here for you . . . to love, to support, to let you know it's okay for you to go."

The sun cracked through the clouds for the first time in days, and light began to fill the room. Céline Dion's "The Power of Love" played. Matt was an encyclopedia of Céline knowledge; she was his grade school obsession before he was introduced to Christina. He held affinities for each diva without needing to compare their talents.

"Smash into You" by Beyoncé. "A New Day" by Céline. "Songbird" by Fleetwood Mac.

Matt and I saw Fleetwood Mac at the Air Canada Centre with Daccia. Matt went into full "woo" mode, which annoyed the people sitting behind us, who refused to stand up. A group of lesbians next to us were inspired by Matt and joined him, further blocking the people behind us. After Lindsay Buckingham shredded a ten-minute guitar solo, Matt turned to me and screamed, "Holy shit, he just had sex with this entire stadium." I fell deeper and deeper in love with him. To love Matt was to sink and relax into adoration, to simmer and thicken with him.

"Elby, it's time. It's time," I coached him. "Just let go. Just like Donna."

The sun erupted across the Toronto skyline, illuminating the autumn leaves of the forest below. The radiant energy bounced an iridescence through the window, bathing us in warm hues. We were golden beings, outlined with saturated pink ribbons, decorated with glints of refracted stainless steel. We were swaddled together in a thick blanket of otherworldly light.

"Oh wow!" I exclaimed. "Oh wow!"

I looked to Angel Eyes standing at the foot of the bed; she was weeping, eyes full of wonder.

"Gentlemen, his time is nearing," said the Doctor. "Don't be afraid to touch him."

I took Matt's right hand, the Boyfriend took his left, and our hands met in the middle. The three of us connected through a shared love.

"I love you, Elby."

"I love you, Matt," said the Boyfriend.

"We love you."

A supernova engulfed the room.

"It's time! It's time! It's time," rings Elaine.

The orchestra kicks up and the audience erupts into thunderous applause. I reach over from the driver's seat and offer Matt my index finger. He wraps his fist tightly around it. He turns off the music and we sit in silence as the windshield wipers squeak across the glass, tears streaming down both our faces.

"You gonna be okay?" he asks.

"Nope," I say. "You? Gonna be okay?"

"Me?" He laughs. "Always."

I sensed the slightest release, a lengthening and contraction of energy, and a stillness overtook the room. My lungs dropped. I inhaled deep the molecules of Matt's final breath.

"I'm sorry. He's gone."

I looked to the clock. The red block numbers read 5:38.

October twenty-ninth, at five thirty-eight.

I pulled away from the bedside and turned to the window. I lifted my hands to my lips and prayed deep and hard to the waning light, bathing in the information as the sky shifted to a vibrant stained-glass ceiling of wild raspberry, electric watermelon, and dark cherry. My prayer was an expression of gratitude for lending me the strength to let go, for the capacity to share this experience with others, for the humanity of the doctors, for the mercy of thirty-eight minutes, and for the grace of nature so vividly expressed. This was the great recalibration, the great reorientation of a one-degree shift. I was permanently altered. This was the gift of being deeply present for your beloved in their most sacred moment.

I turned back to Matt's bedside and stood next to the Boyfriend. I placed my hands on Matt's body, the Boyfriend placed one hand on top of mine. I prayed we would both hold this intimate experience in the weeks to come. The room was still for five minutes, an observance that marks the end of the medical ritual. "Over the Rainbow" by Judy Garland played. We exited the room to see a horseshoe of healthcare workers, salt-stained and mourning. There was no one untouched by the devastation of this young man's passing. They stripped us of our protective gear, they washed our hands with antibacterial gel.

I went to every doctor and nurse present, and I thanked them. "Thank you for your care," over and over. I told the Dad and the

Stepmother. I hugged them and excused myself. I texted the Sister in Australia: "I'm sorry. Matt passed at 5:38. He did not suffer." I pressed send. I walked to the waiting Friends. I repeated over and over, "I'm so sorry." I excused myself and walked away down a hallway. Unsure of where I was going.

Get as far away as possible.

October 29, 2018, 5:38.

Ten, twenty-nine, twenty eighteen, five thirty-eight.

The numbers were like a code unlocking something within.

Matt's birthdate was August 22, 1986.

Eight, twenty-two, nineteen eighty-six.

I began to make a chugging sound, a rolling, heaving, up-and-down noise, like a brick set to tumble dry in the basin of my pelvis. The brick sound grew louder and louder, and I suppressed it by walking faster. I had two hands over an oil geyser. A finger in the crack of a dam.

I passed a doctor typing in her office. She ran after me with her keys in hand. "You," she shouted, unlocking an empty office. "In here. Right now."

"I'm okay. Thank you for your care."

Matt's telephone number was 647-520-7394.

Six-four-seven, five-two-zero, seven-three-nine-four.

I had entered a state of distress but did not know it. I was a ship taking on water unable to signal mayday.

The doctor pulled me into the room.

Born: *zero-eight, two-two, one-nine-eight-six.*

"Stay in here," she ordered, shutting me in. "I'm just outside this door, okay?"

Died: *one-zero, two-nine, two-zero-one-eight, five-three-eight.*

I felt a click and then an unlatching.

I collapsed on the floor. A host of sparrows erupted from my mouth. I was a low string on a cello droning long and deep. My tongue shot up. I was Picasso's *Mother with Dead Child II*. I was *Ally McBeal*, season three, episode sixteen, "Boy Next Door." I was Mother Courage and Arnold Beckoff. My breastbone split and my heart spilled onto the floor. My back arched and my body torqued. I howled and my tears cycled back into my throat.

I bayed over and over again to the fluorescent lights on the ceiling. My lungs billowed and emptied like a church organ until there was no sound left to make.

A satellite view of my body would have shown complete darkness. I was the great blackout, the great earthquake, the great war, a tornado touching down. My grid was offline: transformers blown in geysers of sparks, power lines severed by fallen trees, office towers eroded in half, and highways collapsed into sinkholes. A chain of explosions, one after another, amassing devastation. From space, hovering above gravity, the loss looked like a black void.

Microscopically close, there was a flickering of light. My cells sheltering in place, clasping flashlights and emergency radios, a wave of oxygenated blood rushing towards clouds of ash, search dogs sniffing for life underneath the rubble of calcium. Pulses of Morse code overrode the circuitry of my body: I was a billion missives all reporting life.

I could feel my feet.

The First Two Weeks of
November 2018

I was in shock when I arrived home from the hospital. I had witnessed Matt die in a phenomenon of holy light, but then night came quickly. I sat alone in the dark, the screen of my phone lit up with messages, and I texted a single reply to Daccia: "Fill my home with life." A few breaths later, my front door flew open and friends of every connection entered with food and drink in hand. Heavy fall coats piled on the iron coat rack. It buckled from the weight and ripped off the anchors, dangling skewed. Coats then piled onto my bed. We gathered in a circle, and I told the story of Matt bursting into the sunset. A myth was born, a tale to go where science could not — to describe the synchronicity between the beauty of a sunset and the sorrow of death. We talked about the magnificent sky over Toronto, and how it stopped people in their tracks. Guests passed around their phones with photos of the skyline streaked with gold, magenta, coral, and saffron. "That was Matt." I wept. We stayed up until the early morning talking, flowing from tears to laughter and back.

"This is who shows up for me," I reflected with Cathie, the next day in an emergency session.

I passed her the tissue box as she wept from listening to the story of the man who became light.

Then began a breakup in reverse as two years of separation immediately evaporated, time looped, and the cat arrived back at my doorstep. It felt like watching a clip of an impact event backwards as the fallout re-forms into buildings. I took ownership in the care of Stevie. This was the only time I asserted myself with all of those in attendance at the hospital. The cat was my responsibility: she became my ward. Stevie circled the perimeter of the apartment, opening cupboard doors with her paw and sniffing at doorjambs before settling as if nothing happened on the mid-century armchair she had clawed up years before. Only now, I didn't care if she picked at the upholstery; I felt petty for the arguments she'd spurred between Matt and me.

With the cat back at home, every piece of furniture in the apartment had heightened meaning. The dresser Matt bought me for my birthday, the footstool he sat on on Sunday mornings while combing the cat, the rope lamp we pulled from the basement of a church rummage sale — these were touchstones activated by death. Time slowed and blended with colorful holograms as I slipped between tenses and wrote his obituary at the kitchen table. Matt chased me around the house ort-orting like a seal while I whinnied like a horse, and I sat recording the action with a pen and yellow legal pad. I began to tell his story and started the process of speaking and writing about him using the past tense while watching him in the present. *He was terrified of June bugs and would scream "Juneys" and swat the air at the sight. He was never without lip balm in his right-hand pocket. His guiding philosophy was "Never disturb a settled cat." He was a lover of chocolate caramel balls and dino-sour candies, breakfast for dinner, and would successfully debate that baked nachos were a complete meal representing all four food groups.* Nostalgic visions didn't soothe the bitter taste of the word *was* as I read his obituary aloud.

The sixteen-hour drive to Quispamsis, Matt's hometown, began with collecting his ashes from a Toronto funeral home. The white cardboard box with an identification label was so surprisingly heavy that I nearly dropped it as it was handed to me. Matt had "unusually high bone mass and density — even for someone his age and size." This information didn't surprise me: he was a broad, hardy man in perfect health. I understood the funeral director's trade notes as a compliment of Matt's physique. Matt was vain, in a balanced way, and he would have bragged that his cremation yielded an excessive amount of ashes. When the director politely asked how Matt died, I told her the tale of the man who became the sun. I held her hand as she cried; I told this stranger with no connection to Matt that it was okay.

This was my new role — I became that person who said, "Don't worry. It's okay."

I brought Matt home so that Stevie could have her goodbye. The Maine Coon sniffed around the box, rubbed her chin on the corner, and stretched out beside Matt. After she walked away, I placed him in a leather satchel with a blue linen lining. I buckled the satchel into the passenger seat of my rental car, and Matt sat beside me the entire trip. It was more ceremonial than convenient to travel by land; we had driven the province-by-province route several times together. When I stopped at a rest stop, I slung him over my shoulder. When I stopped overnight in Ottawa at my cousin's apartment, I placed him in a chair at the foot of the bed. When I went through a Tim Hortons drive-thru deep in northern Quebec, I asked him if he wanted anything before placing an order in broken French. We sat beside the Saint Lawrence River on a breakwater in the village of Saint-Jean-Port-Joli and I released in sorrow. I phoned a friend and asked them to be that person who just says, "It's okay."

Matt's memorial was held at the Shadow Lawn Inn, an elegant white and gray manor home on the Kennebecasis River, outside Saint John, New Brunswick. It was a Dragonfly Inn—esque venue with adjoining rooms for guests to collect and gather. The front lobby was filled with stunning floral arrangements sent from across the country and a large photo of Matt. A slideshow of his life cycled in the dining room, with finger foods and coffee service. Matt's immediate family organized a tasteful celebration of life. I didn't contribute to the planning, as I understood my role was to represent the decade after he left his small-town community to study classical theater in Toronto.

At the reception, I was a floating receiving line as I met his public school teachers, the childhood friends, the neighbors, the mothers who let him watch Disney movies in their basements. I finally met Matt's Italian uncles, aunts, and cousins. They were the relatives I was most curious about, the ancestry that he had emotionally cordoned off from our relationship. I had accepted an entire heritage nonchalantly, but in meeting his relatives and shaking their hands it put into focus that Matt was genuinely Italian. I saw Matt in their features. I asked his zia about his nonna's cooking, about the gnocchi recipe, the family basement filled with vintage treasures — dry commonalities for his relatives that had held such an emotional life for Matt. He'd carried such nostalgia for his Italian family, for his mother and her parents — all predeceased.

I started developing a script, short and quick statements to navigate the grief of others. "His passing was quick and he did not suffer." "We shared six beautiful years together as partners and two more as family." I reunited with Matt's extended East Coast family, the exuberant aunts and uncles and loving cousins with big personalities. These were his primary relationships growing up and the people he bore the most resemblance to physically and in character. They were first on the imaginary guest list for the wedding that had still been a question in the back of his aunts' minds. "We wanted to grow old together, but didn't know how or what that would look like," I added to the script.

Matt and I could never wrap our heads around our wedding. Marriage was a running topic in our relationship. Once, we ate dinner at a west-end diner and thought this is how we'd do it: rent out a restored diner and fill the tiny booths with a few of our closest friends. But then we started to chip away at the interpersonal dynamics. We couldn't fathom the celebration and who to include (and not include) to make it work — especially with my estranged family. We knew that our first dance would be choreographed to the *Law & Order: SVU* theme song, but it was easier to deny ourselves the experience than figure it out.

I looked around the venue, thinking, *Why aren't weddings more like funerals? Events of radical inclusion where people show up, compelled to honor their connection, moved to honor a life?* The communal experience of sharing an anecdote, the vulnerability of an emotional memory, and a messy expression of how they loved and felt loved by the deceased was beautiful. It was revealing to recognize a life as a series of fragmented units, stitched together as part of a larger whole. Everyone in attendance lovingly held a piece of Matt for each other.

I saw the totality of Matt, a partner I thought I once knew inside and out. (The feeling was mutual: Matt once joked in a birthday card, "I know your smells.") Matt was his mother's high school friend, his university theater mentor Ilkay, his friends Kelsey and Amy, the redheaded family two doors away from his childhood home. Matt was his many cousins, aunts, and uncles. Matt was Louisa and Daccia. Matt was his boyfriend and Toronto friends. The gathering was the fullest expression of him. In death, the gift was the opportunity to witness that assembly and to participate by holding a stranger's hand, offering them a moment of comfort with a hug, or to stand with them beside his remains now placed in a wooden chest surrounded by family photos and flowers on a table of honor.

Matt was very much present, but within hours, after the last guest left, even that essence of him vanished from my life.

Late that night, after many a glass of wine with the cousins, I returned to the cottage I'd rented for the duration of my stay. The place was owned by a hoarder who reminded me of Anne Ramsey, the actress who played Mama Fratelli in *The Goonies*. She was a gruff but nice woman who laughed when I asked if there was a key to the place. She noted in a thick East Coast accent that she had a key but lost it in 1975. I just wanted a good view and privacy. The front room overlooked the water system that connects to the Saint John River and flows into the Bay of Fundy. The bay is noted for having the highest tides in the world; also, from personal experience, it has the coldest water my body has plunged into.

I needed a lot of space — away from the community that had gathered in the basement of Matt's childhood home. I needed a place where I could drink the bottle of Bulleit purchased from a Fredericton gas station and not be judged. I didn't want to have to hide the fact that anything other than alcohol, caffeine, or sugar made me dart to the washroom. Nobody told me that I would lose ten pounds as my body rejected anything that wasn't salty, fatty, or sweet. I drove halfway across Canada on two bagels.

I sat eating a discount jumbo styro-pack tray of Gagnon pecan caramels and scrolled through my phone. An avalanche of emails and check-ins. Early on I started replying with a single prayer hands emoji. Half of the messages and missed calls were from David. We had not spoken since he'd called in response to my emergency text. My phone lit up with an incoming call. It was David — again. I closed my eyes and contemplated whether it was a good choice to answer his call. The gap between us was now a time difference of four hours. I answered before the voicemail kicked in and poured myself another drink.

"Hello."

"Where are you?"

"New Brunswick. You?"

"I'm in LA." His voice was strained. "You okay?"

"No, David, I'm not okay."

"Are you safe?"

"I've been very well cared for."

"Did you read my —"

"No."

"This is a lot," David said.

"This is a lot?" I tucked myself into an alcove down the hallway of Sunnybrook's D-wing and steadied my back against the wall.

"What do you want me to do?"

"Fly to Toronto."

"It's too much."

"I'll pay for the flight. I don't care about money."

"No. It's too much."

"What's too much?"

"This."

"This is too much for you?"

David paused. I could hear him centering himself on the other end. "I'm driving up to San Francisco to see the Mountain this weekend."

We called this new man the Mountain because David's enthusiasm seemed insurmountable and, for me, the climb was not worth the energy. The Mountain was closeted. As an advanced homosexual, you don't need to fuck a ripe peach to know how that relationship ends. I mentally gave it six weeks before it was over.

"David. I'm hanging up the phone, but not because you're seeing someone new — I couldn't give a fuck. I'm hanging up because you're an asshole."

"Shawn, don't speak to me like this."

I unleashed my attack dog.

"No, David. You wanted a fucking Matt deal. You aren't worthy of a Matt deal. You certainly aren't willing to earn it. Don't call me, don't text, don't write. Go back to Instagramming your fucking matching Birkenstock sandals on the beach. I'm done with this roller-coaster. I have to go take my ex-husband off life support. I have greater concerns than your romantic patterns."

"Shawn, don't hang —"

"Can we talk?"

"I can't do a deep dive, David. I'm raw. I haven't eaten in two weeks, and I'm drunk."

"No deep dive. I just want to hear your voice."

"I've been talking all day. Tell me what you're looking at."

"I'm standing in front of a vegan taco stand in Highland Park."

"That sounds really lovely."

"Weird, you were supposed to be here today."

"I could say the same for you."

On the final day before all the delegates departed, we gathered in the family living room for a communal breakfast. The bouquets, cards, and decorations from the venue were tucked in corners and cascaded off side tables and pooled on the floor. I ate the edge of a baked egg casserole and chewed on perfectly cooked bacon. I still had one last night before driving back, with a planned extended layover in Montreal for further quiet time. The conversation was light, and we slipped in and out of laughter. The CBC's Remembrance Day service began playing in the background, and the living room went silent. It cut through the laughter and story-telling, and all our heads bowed without prompt. I heard in my body the words of "In Flanders Fields" by John McCrae.

We are the Dead. Short days ago
We lived, felt dawn, saw sunset glow,
Loved and were loved . . .

I knew not the horrors of war but the swiftness of death, the guilt of still feeling the sun on my face. The mourning we shared connected to a historical grief. I inhaled as the bugle played "Last Post," and we sat observing two minutes of silence. I looked across the room at Matt's dad, a man who understood sorrow. He'd lost his first wife and now his son. My heart shattered into a billion more pieces.

The most comforting moments while in Quispamsis were the ones spent with Matt's dad. The walk around the subdivision, pushing his infant grandson in a stroller. The car ride to the cemetery to visit the plot where Matt would rest. The office where we pored over Matt's estate. Matt's dad spoke to me from a place of knowing. As if someone had sat him down in the face of grief and offered their wisdom. It was an inheritance that I was given. Perhaps he recognized the pain I wore, and that, in combination with my history and connection with his son, outweighed any nomenclature.

We were on the way back into town after dinner with Matt's firecracker grandma. I felt a great sense of duty to visit her before I left, to let her know that her grandson did not suffer. As I drove us through unlit back-country roads, Matt's dad copiloted me through the sharp bends that followed the coastline and looked like dead ends in the high beams. We found a balance between tenderness and humor that reminded me of my car rides with Louisa's husband, George. I found myself intentionally driving well under the speed limit to lengthen our time together.

"All I ever wanted was for my son to be happy," he said.

"He found such joy and happiness in his life. You remain an incredible dad."

"I'm sure your father wants the same for you — just watch out for deer up ahead."

Two weeks had passed, and my father had yet to call or text his condolences. Messages from David continued to collect in my pocket. A wave of doom for my future relationships washed over me. I worried that my past ill-equipped me for happiness in the future, and it was my destiny to struggle to connect with men. Matt was my constant: as long as I could maintain a balanced connection with him, then I knew I had one person in this lifetime who loved me without condition, who showed up. I was about to leave the ashes of that love on an occasional table in the corner of a living room and make the long drive home.

"I would hope," I replied. "But Matt and I had very different experiences. That was the gift of Matt: he could carry all my jagged bits and pieces."

"Just stay away from the bottle, don't dwell, and keep moving forward."

"I'll try."

Matt's passing was a tart pomegranate seed. A tiny bit of knowing that I innocently swallowed and now carry inside me for the rest of my life.

I witnessed a metamorphosis when he transitioned. Greek poets wove tragic tales of lovers who changed physical forms, transforming in death into wonders of nature. How else to explain events that reason or science fails to, if not in a symbolic language that bridges our understanding of life's mysteries. Logic could not soothe the loss of Matt. The numinous experience left me mumbling the word *grace*.

Grace felt spacious. Grace offered comfort.

Days after returning from Matt's memorial in New Brunswick, I sat at a dining table, petting a cat, and talking about grace with a clergywoman. I had met Reverend Christine while performing at a fundraiser for an LGBTQ youth support group organized by her parish. Christine held the unique qualification of a PhD in theology with a dissertation on comedy and religion.

My parents raised me without religion — for this I am truly thankful. We lived next to a church, and my father would refrain from cutting the front lawn on Sunday mornings; that was the extent of my family's religious tolerance. We were farmers: nature was our greatest teacher, common sense our guide. As a kid, I was quickly kicked out of bible school (read: free babysitting) for challenging the story of Jesus pushing an enormous boulder to free himself from a tomb after resurrection.

"Wait. No. Go back," I interrupted the teacher. "To the rock part. Let me get this straight: he's just come back from the dead, and he has the strength to push a boulder? How did he get out of the tomb?"

"He just did!" argued the teacher.

"Impossible!" I demanded logic.

Being excommunicated held no weight when I only attended for the crafting sessions, orange drink, and guitar sing-alongs.

When Reverend Christine asked me my thoughts on Christianity, I deflected. "What if God is asparagus?"

I told her what I witnessed in the hospital room, we spoke about the resurrection of Jesus Christ, and we held hands as Christine led us in prayer for Matthew. It was the most welcome I'd ever felt towards a faith, and I was able to have a capacious conversation about religion. Then I wept at her kitchen table because I didn't know if you could still be a comedian, be queer, and believe in God.

I used to mock those who believed in God. Large parts of myself have been closed off to belief, and for good reason. Religion continues its shameful legacy of being an unsafe space for queers. How many marginalized people have been harmed by the weaponizing of belief? How do the empires of faith continue to profit by policing othered bodies, our communities, and the physical expressions of our love? Their ideology has cauterized our soothing instincts, denied a human birthright to comfort and to symbolic language. Opening ourselves to belief means beginning the painful work of reconciling the parts of ourselves that have been amputated or walled off in self-protection.

Healing is the restoration of one's creativity.

I do not ascribe to any theology, but I no longer label myself an atheist. I don't need to know how Jesus got out of the tomb: I hold space for the unknown without demanding answers. My practice is to believe in something, anything — whatever stories take shape, to let them be as vivid, outrageous, and life-giving as the ancient myths.

I believe we are gifted one body in this life. I believe the spirit is contained in the body and becomes disembodied when you die. I believe the soul is energy and therefore indestructible. I believe that to harm the body in an attempt to destroy another's spirit is to violate the sacred. Like Plutarch, I believe that to know what is sacred is to do no harm. Like Ovid, I believe love is the only constant in life and death. I believe in nature's grace and intelligent design. I believe orchids are a symbol of adaptation, resilience, and patience. I believe in the perfect geometry of a honeycomb, a dahlia, a pinecone, a conch shell. I believe in science and math, I believe in God. I believe God is asparagus who reveals itself for two weeks a year in Southern Ontario before going to seed.

I believe that Matt transformed into light when he left this life.

End of November 2018

Weighted cutlery rested on beautifully pressed cotton napkins; silver chargers cradled large white plates, and a truffle marked midnight at the top of each place setting. The white painted dining room table looked like a surreal landscape. To the right of my untouched water glass, merely acting as moral support for my wine goblet, rested a small brass-tone vintage windmill. It was a relic of Matt's childhood, something that transported him to joy. I remembered when Matt pulled it out from a crawlspace in his parents' basement, grinning as he spun the sails with his index finger. It now joined the parade of miniature bric-a-brac that decorated the center of the table in a theatrical tableau, and the scale between the objects set a humorous tone for the evening. The collection included a vintage figurine of a man in an orange jumpsuit wearing a blue dunce cap with faded yellow stars, a green marble frog, a white ornamental pumpkin, and five-barrel keys strung together with satin blue ribbon. These were the fanciful elements set for the feast of abbondanza.

Amanda, Matt's sister, was the guest of honor. She was radiant; her features were similar to her brother's, only delicate. She was seated in Matt's chair, bouncing her five-month-old son on her lap. Daccia circled the table clockwise, refreshing our glasses from a chilled bottle of white wine. I didn't have to indicate — Daccia knowingly filled mine to the rim. The steady flow of wine softened the cruel twist of fate of Matt's death, the heavy-handed course correction that had prevented me from floating away from this table.

Amanda listened to the stories of her brother. How he ate radishes like tiny apples leaving a core and root on his plate like disemboweled mice. How Matt often hit his head on the low-hanging chandelier as he entered Louisa's home. How we all sang the word *cassoulet* to the tune of Enya's "Orinoco Flow." How it was custom to discuss the weekly dilemma in the *New York Times*'s ethics column. *Cas-sou-let, cas-sou-let, cas-sou-let.* How in the political debates Matt was always the voice of positivity. *Cas-sou-let, cas-sou-let, cas-sou-let.* The night the New York City family flew in and we drank eight different bottles of bourbon dry. *Cas-sou-let, cas-sou-let, cas-sou-let.* These were the stories that glued our city family together.

I was at a point beyond exhaustion, past the delirium of ecstatic dance and temper tantrums of children. I'd ignored my inner warning system, that crack in my chest that signaled impending emotional disintegration. *Just make it through dinner.* Amanda and I had spent three days cleaning out Matt's apartment. We arrived in time for dinner, unwashed and numb. Matt's belongings were safely tucked away in Louisa's garage until they could be re-homed or shipped to New Brunswick. The smell of tomato sauce from the kitchen threatened to tip me over into tears of hunger. I have not eaten in a month, and my doctor said it was "only" natural. It was only natural to consume the bare minimum, only natural to bypass taste buds, only natural to swallow. My blood was a crimson syrup of sugar, caffeine, and wine.

Louisa entered from the kitchen, holding a ceramic trough overflowing with pasta, roast chicken quarters, and braised fennel.

"I'm afraid it's just simple fare tonight," Louisa said, placing the giant bowl on the table.

My eyes flooded with tears as my appetite escaped me.

Eighteen Sundays had passed since my fight with Louisa, but something was different — other than the obvious departure. Amanda's presence softened the blow of Matt's absence, a sort of weaning process for future dinners without him. Matt was here by proxy. I saw his dark eyes, brown hair, and full smile when I looked at his nephew. I saw Matt's framed obituary photo beside George's on the credenza in the foyer. He was not missing — the man of honor was everywhere. A film of dust made from his skin cells covered my body; he was caked in my clothes and lodged in my sinuses. His lips once kissed the napkins on our laps and the edges of the glassware. He was the windmill in the center. I reached over and began fidgeting with the trinket, my thumb pad tracing the raised edges of the stamped details. I spun the metal sail and it rattled. I scanned the room like a detective. *What the fuck are you looking for?* The centerpiece on the table and the mantle: all the taper candles and votive tea lights had been swapped out for flickering battery-operated LEDs. Salon lighting without the lingering scent of expired sulfur or the hiss of a wet wick cracking softly through molten wax.

"I really need to pee," Amanda said. "I just can't go in there."

She stood outside the doorway to the bathroom, holding her son. The bathroom was the site of Matt's accident, the cramped galley where his homemade costume caught the edge of a lit candle.

"I just don't understand how it happened? It just doesn't make sense. How?"

Her emotional needs were trumping her immediate physical needs.

"What if that is the grace we've been offered?" I asked.

"How do you mean?" She broke her study of the room.

"What if we're not supposed to know? What if we were spared that knowledge? What if it's not for us to carry? It's not part of our healing."

"Well, that's a way of looking at it." Amanda looked at me, slightly annoyed — I was a bit too airy for Matt's family.

"This bathroom is not how Matt died. Matt died surrounded by love and care."

She paused. "Okay! Here —" Amanda passed over her son. "Hold him."

I walked down the hallway into the living room, bouncing Matt's nephew in my arms. I didn't need to speculate about how the accident transpired. I knew based on my deductive reasoning and my understanding of Matt. The apartment told the story. There were lighters, matchbooks, and tea light candles stashed in drawers in every room. On every ledge and table, he placed vintage ashtrays, votive holders, and pillar candles.

Smoke detectors without batteries were under sinks and in the back of closets. I suspected they had been taken down when he painted and never put back up. He had a plan to rehang them. Matt always had a plan, but like doing the dishes after cooking, his timeline could lack a sense of urgency. To be Matt's partner was to rehang the smoke detectors, to replace the batteries yearly, to wash the sheets weekly, to dig out the cat litter daily. To be Matt's partner was to be the rock grounding a helium balloon. Matt wasn't negligent, accident-prone, or clumsy; he held a different relationship to stress that made him less responsive to hazards. The fun, gregarious, easy-going personality that everyone cherished had a consequential offshoot that I had felt the need to manage. It was the extra responsibility of caregiving lovingly performed by me, the stick in the mud who didn't allow candles in our apartment.

Walking into the burn unit of the hospital, I knew I was in a lose-lose situation. In a scenario where the prognosis would have resulted in life, I would have been a primary caregiver in Matt's long and painful recovery — there was no question. I would have dedicated the rest of my life to supporting Matt. But with Matt's death came a weighted freedom as I held on to a semblance of my life. Now I saw colors as deeply saturated and vibrant. Every coffee, laugh, dynamic sunset I experienced with penitence. I was only beginning to comprehend this growing burden of contrast as survivor's guilt.

Matt had tied me into his estate after we separated. I didn't know, but it didn't surprise me. We were still each other's emergency contacts, we remained family, we made morbid jokes about Matt receiving my pittance residual checks if I should croak first. In making me his next of kin, Matt saved me from being cast as some grim Mary Poppins character who appeared at the hospital, supported an end-of-life procedure, and then disappeared into the wind. The person I served was Matt, his needs and desires. Although this was my first experience in doing post-death work, I knew instinctually that we honor the dead by sorting, folding, boxing, and bagging in service to a life lived. We do it with a sense of duty and the knowledge that the healing work is not to finish, fix, correct, or override, but to cleanse, scrub, lift, sweat, and sweep while in conversation about your beloved.

Amanda returned and we continued the intimate task. I felt very comfortable around her — as if she were my own sister. We were almost the same age (Matt was six years our junior), and we both shed our former wild child personalities in adulthood. We'd bonded one summer in Halifax when I stayed with her for two weeks while performing at a festival. The first week we stayed up late talking on the back porch, eating Covered Bridge potato chips and drinking beer. On the second, Matt flew out and the three of us took a day trip to Lunenburg, ate dinners with their cousin, and danced drunkenly to The Weeknd until the early morning. I felt a great sense of duty towards her. I carried the burden of being the one to tell her not to fly to Toronto to see Matt before he died, in order to spare him the wait and further suffering. She flew directly to New Brunswick from Australia. Cleaning out the apartment was Amanda's opportunity to say goodbye to her baby brother, to touch the things he'd last touched, to preserve the relics of his life, to anoint heirlooms for the next generation of her family.

"When your brother moved in with me," I reminisced while tossing a handful of chopsticks into a garbage bag, "I showed up with a moving truck, and he had all of his things in garbage bags sitting in the back alley. I told him the objective of moving was to not look like you're being evicted. That it was a choice to uproot yourself."

She laughed. "Yup, sounds like Matt."

Donation boxes in the front room began to pile up, and black garbage bags heaped higher and higher. It was the multiples of everyday objects, that extra container of Comet or hair pomade, that held the absurdity of assuming one had a future. It wasn't the airplane ticket to France, or the master's degree program he was to apply for that spoke to the unfairness of death. Heartbreak was the economy-sized bag of Unico pastina stored beside boxes of chicken bouillon cubes and dried rosemary. It was the future plans he made to prepare a bowl of his nonna's soup at any point, to be comforted by a family recipe. A heritage remedy for those moments when he felt glum, conflicted, or the onset of a chill.

A formal dinner creates a lot of room for pretense. No one at this table was pretending. There was permission to be vulnerable, unlike before. "Can I be emotionally honest with you?" is an unspoken foundational question that tests the strength of a family beyond bloodlines. We checked our social graces at the front door and, with that buffer removed, I understood this family as real. We broke bread, five individuals each with unique ties to a life that had senselessly evaporated.

Pretending was the thorn in my gut that had spurred my fight with Louisa. Our childish rift ended the moment I informed her of the accident. It was my phone call to make, and the exchange was primal. Louisa was about to lose a son, someone she nurtured, fed, and overpraised for nearly a decade. His home was filled with artifacts of their relationship, expressions of her love offered through gifts that developed his taste buds and his interest (*The Essential Collection: Maria Callas*, a rose gold designer watch, *Blood, Bones & Butter* by Gabrielle Hamilton). Louisa's paintings hung on his walls, and tiny drawn caricatures of his likeness were sprinkled throughout his belongings.

"Is everything okay with the food?" Louisa noticed me picking slowly at my plate.

"Yes. It's absolutely delicious. I'm just taking my time."

"More wine, Shawn?" Daccia gently steered.

"Please."

Daccia passed the bottle over the heatless candles. I tipped the spout into Amanda's glass, then finished the bottle in mine. *He kept all the love letters, the drawings, the mementos, the gifts. He kept the weird clown noses you wore around the house.*

I looked down at my black hoodie; I brushed at the fabric with my free hand. I was covered in cat hair. "This is going to take time to get used to."

"How is Stevie?" asked Daccia.

"She's fine," I guessed. "Just lounging around as if nothing happened."

"She's so cute," Louisa complimented. "Must be nice to have her home."

Switch gears.

"Do you remember immediately after George died?" I asked.

That's switching gears? Bringing up the dead so cavalierly was not taboo — we included memories of Louisa's husband as a constant thread in our conversations.

"The four of us were all standing around the island in the kitchen. Just destroyed," I said. "Matt had arrived from work. He didn't know what to say, so he told us . . ."

"That," Daccia picked up, "earlier in the day he accidentally tweeted that he sharted himself at the office."

"Yes! He thought he'd sent a private message to his friend." I laughed.

"And he left it up for hours on his timeline." Daccia cackled.

"Do I remember?" Louisa interjected. "Here I am, having lost my husband of thirty-plus years. And I have my three kids rolling on the floor, laughing like lunatics."

Amanda laughed. "Yup, that sounds like my brother."

Matt was tidy, but he was not a cleaner. I whisked large tumbleweeds of cat fur across the floor of his attic bedroom with a broom. These formations were "Stevie balls," and if you gathered enough, you could roll them together, glue on two googly eyes, and chase each other around the house with the creature. He was drawn to rickety old spaces with uneven floors and cracked plaster. He didn't mind a damp smell or sticky linoleum tiles. His first Cabbagetown apartment should have been condemned. The windows were nailed closed and it was full of hidden nooks crammed with hardcore pornography left by the previous tenants. If a space looked haunted or about to fall over, Matt wanted to nest in it. He created a warm sense of home with objects he found rummaging through church basements or pulled from the curbside trash. If something had gold plating, a beveled edge, or a pewter finish, it was coming home.

I knew the provenance of a headboard, a wool rug, a set of salt-and-pepper shakers. I could date the child's handwriting on a carrot cake recipe and how it ended up being passed from Louisa and Daccia's family to Matt. I knew the story of a vintage topographical map of France bought in Parkdale. It was the first piece of art that Matt purchased, and expensive, for us. Matt was drawn to its orange, blue, and emerald green. The brittle map, hung slightly too high, didn't tell the story of us circling up Roncesvalles, across Dundas, down Lansdowne, and back four times while deciding to put it on a credit card. Two mid-century side tables were a memory of a day trip to Uxbridge to visit one of our teak dealers. Some gay couples have coke dealers; Matt and I had teak dealers, jam ladies, and fudge connections.

I felt like a hard drive containing a volume of knowledge of Matt's life as I told Amanada about the idiosyncrasies of her brother. He had an anthology of Meryl Streep movies that he watched to force himself to emote, his "cry-tear-ion" collection. He was deeply sentimental and kept a box filled with cards, concert tickets, lanyards, and programs. Matt and I each kept one and labeled them our "death boxes." He loved whimsy and positioned miniatures and tiny figurines on ledges or in crannies. A framed poster had a tiny red London phone booth balanced on the top right-hand corner. Above a doorjamb sat a thumb-sized porcelain cow's skull. An owl named Hoot-Hoot lived in the kitchen cupboard with his mugs. The pewter figurine greeted him every time he made tea or coffee. Old tins, a wooden donkey, and brass clawfoot were all part of his mythological world he assembled. He transported himself to another realm by feeling the smoothness of a wood grain, the braille pits of rust, the coldness of marble. It was these journeys of touch that led him to the town where he was mayor and it was always twenty-three degrees and sunny (but not too sunny).

Some would label the behavior dissociative. Sure, it was alarming to come home and catch your partner standing in the corner singing in his head, lip-syncing to an imaginary track and using a reading lamp he pulled from the garbage as a microphone. Yes, it was hilarious to see him locked in a trance for extended periods while brushing his chin and lips with a blue silicone basting brush. Matt was a kooky pathfinder, and I adored his creative ways of self-regulating. I cherished being there to greet him as he arrived back to reality.

"I don't understand how you're doing this," Amanda said.

"I did it for years." I smiled. "Thursdays mornings I did laundry while he was at work. I cooked. I cleaned. I loved it."

She watched from the edge of the bed while I began to fold Matt's clothes for the last time — probably the most intimate chore. His clothes were a part of his self-expression. Matt knew how to dress, he took pride in his appearance, and he loved a compliment. With each item I pulled from the closet or dresser, I offered my gratitude. I silently gave thanks to the pair of jeans, floral dress shirt, or chunky knit sweater for the comfort and protection they'd offered Matt. For their help in expressing his radiant personality. My gratitude became silent messages in the envelopes of cloth I was making, fold by fold. Stacked in blue recycling bags for donation, clothes, shoes, and hats were the remnants of Matt that would soon find their way into thrift stores around Toronto for second or third lives. He would be spread out and incorporated in the wardrobes of other men. If I walked down the street in the upcoming months and saw a T-shirt or pair of winter boots from these bags, would I even recognize them as Matt's?

❧❧

Daccia made her way west after we said good night on the street. I helped Amanda and the nephew get into a waiting car of the family Amanda was staying with. We had one more day at the apartment to wrap up before saying goodbye. We hugged and I squeezed the nephew's hand one last time. I waved as the car drove off down the street, until the red taillights turned south and out of sight.

I reentered Louisa's home. The ongoing nightmare of November hit. I asked to sit down for a couple minutes before heading home. I sat numb on the steps of the sunken foyer; my shoes wet from outside darkened an antique Turkish rug. Louisa brought over a glass of water and sat close beside me. She placed her hand lovingly on my back. A wave of sadness escaped my body and I turned into her tiny frame. She cradled my full adult weight as if I were her own: a mother who had lost a son, holding a son who had lost his husband. I sobbed into her apron like a baby with colic.

"He's gone. He's just stuff. He's bowls and shoes and dust. My husband is gone." I cried.

"It's okay. It's okay," Louisa cooed. "It's all going to be okay."

"He kept all of it. I found the love letters, the cards, the drawings. Everything."

"I know. I know."

"How did you do that with George? All those years."

"Do what?"

"Clean out his stuff!"

"We just do it for our loves."

"Matt could make me do anything. I never want to do that again."

The word *never* growled off the back of my throat as I shook my head like a stubborn toddler.

"My dear, dear child. Don't you worry. You won't ever have to do that again."

Matt slept through the devastating 2013 ice storm that crystallized then shattered Toronto's tree canopy. I watched with the cat from the living room window as, one by one, toppling branches crushed cars and downed wires. The sound of trees cracking was ominous and resonant, like moans from the roots, the toes of trees cemented in frozen earth. When the hydro went out, I looked over to the fridge, frustrated that the ingredients for our first Christmas dinner away from our families would soon spoil.

In the morning, Matt woke up and said that the streets looked like dismembered arms wearing opera gloves made from ice. I opened the windows to the spare bedroom to create an ersatz walk-in fridge. For two days, Matt and I (and the cat) huddled underneath two duvets in our winter coats. Matt was determined to have a proper Christmas morning. He wasn't upset or annoyed — he just made the best of the situation by eating cookies and making light of our karma for trying to start our own couple's tradition. Come the morning of the twenty-fifth, the Christmas tree lights blinked on and the fridge started buzzing. Our building's core temperature began to rise, and we were able to open our gifts without wearing our puffy coats or seeing our breath.

We moved to the couch and spooned under the duvets while the cat roosted at our feet. Our unspoiled turkey roasted in the oven, filling our home with warmth. Matt's body radiated heat, and I had never been more thankful for having someone to love during the darkest and coldest days of the year.

That first Christmas after Matt died was more challenging than I imagined it would be.

I could feel micro spikes of ice crystallizing over my pores, and my chest contracted tight with every thought of celebrating. With Matt, I learned to cherish the holiday, and Christmas became a Fezziwig extravaganza. Now the season felt weaponized, like it was an opportunity for the universe to highlight the contrast between how I should feel and my despair. In the Advent weeks, I couldn't tolerate the saccharine carols playing in stores, or conceive of opening the box of vintage ornaments (every glass bulb a time bomb of memory), or muster the energy to cook and entertain guests on Christmas Eve. I wanted to sleep through it and wake up in the new year.

While coming home from the yoga studio, I saw an evergreen sapling tossed in a snowbank. Harvested before its prime and discarded days before the solstice, the undesirable tree had five or so branches. Its arms were not strong enough to hold a single ornament. I pulled it from the snowbank and gave it a fair shake before bringing it inside the apartment. I popped it in a mason jar filled with fresh water. I pulled out the Christmas light strings and laid them on the hardwood floor in a circle around it to make a wreath of light. I took the best photos of Matt and clipped them to the tree branches with wooden clothes-pegs. I stood back and softened. "O Grief-mas tree, O Grief-mas tree! How lovely are thy branches," I sang aloud before bursting into laughter.

A little bit of light entered the apartment, where it glowed in the darkest corner. I felt the illumination of my screen as I messaged a handful of friends and offered my home for Christmas Eve. Then the fridge light became a beacon for the makings of a small feast. I cleaned the apartment and rehung the coat rack by the front door.

Days later the guests arrived. Louisa brought the champagne, and Daccia brought the cheesecake. I served a sausage and chestnut risotto, a roasted spatchcocked turkey with a bacon lattice, and an arugula salad: simple fare. Laughter warmed the apartment, glasses were refilled, and Stevie appeared donning her yuletide collar. Will, Daccia's new artist beau, handed me a gift. I was more than embarrassed that I had nothing to offer him in return. Inside, a framed hand-drawn portrait of Matt; his likeness brought him immediately into the festivities. It was the most beautiful Christmas gift I had ever received. My faithful friends gathered even nearer and supported me as I broke down in grief once more.

"Something's not right this year," I said after the tender moment.

"Honey, it's because Matt's gone," said a childhood friend.

"No. Why are we doing this on Christmas Eve?"

"Because you said to come over Christmas Eve," remarked another friend.

"But we always gather on Christmas Day!" I realized.

"We know!" said Daccia.

"Well, what the hell are you all doing tomorrow?"

"We have nothing planned. We always come to your place."

"Well, let's do this again!" I said.

"Come over to my place!" Louisa offered.

Laughter erupted in the apartment, and merriment returned. Then, on Christmas Day, we gathered again and I arrived at Louisa's bearing leftovers.

Christmas, the solstice, Saturnalia, Kwanzaa, Hanukkah (although based on the lunar cycle) are traditions of celebrating the light, restoring the balance, and softening in the coldest and darkest moments of life. We gather in communities around symbols that orient us towards the light, and often we speak of miracles. For me, the miracle of that first Christmas was finding a disappointing and abandoned tree that I anointed as sacred. It meant finding the light at the start of a long and cold Canadian winter and holding the knowledge that the days get longer and brighter, almost imperceptibly, each day until the equinox.

We are always promised a spring.

BONES

March 30, 2019

We sat on a grassy mound dotted with tiny white flowers by Lake Merritt. A gentle spring breeze cooled our backs as we ignored a jazz-funk trio playing in the nearby bandstand. After a morning hike in Tilden Regional Park, David and I refueled with pulled pork sandwiches and USA-sized Greek salads that were beds of red onions sprinkled with olives, tomato, and feta. We enjoyed the sunshine before seeing a matinee at the Grand Lake Theatre, whose large vaudeville roof sign sat like a neon crown over the quaint skyline of Oakland; the street-level marquee condemned the recent mosque shootings in Christchurch alongside the Saturday movie listings. We hadn't discussed world politics or anything outside ourselves; we were pretzeled into a conversation of knots knotted upon knots. Since I'd landed in the Bay Area the previous night, we had picked and pulled, trying to untangle a long yarn of confusion like Vladimir and Estragon.

"Do you think any of your behavior could be described as manic?" I asked David in a moment of calm.

"I don't feel like being pathologized," David snapped.

"I'm not pathologizing you." I spoke as clearly and sternly as I could.

Our three days together were planned, over the winter months, as a quick flight up the coast to enjoy each other's company and to reconnect while holding a question of us. It was a weekend away during my trip to Los Angeles, where I was exploring neighborhoods and getting the lay of the land, devising a new life plan that now included an adult cat. The Toronto winter had been particularly dreadful, and I found myself able to breathe in LA without the chokehold of grief. Let out from the container of my Toronto apartment, where every surface, furniture piece, fork, and poster held a memory of Matt, I felt provisionally released from my sorrow. I felt human riding Lyft scooters through Mar Vista, swimming in a saltwater pool, eating dollar tacos out of the back of a Ford pickup, sightseeing in Venice, and accidentally buying sixteen-dollar pints of organic strawberries while on the phone with David. But now I was back in a claustrophobic box, trying to figure out what was going on with him.

Asking David if he felt manic wasn't me being flip. I'd charted his actions over the winter months through our daily check-ins. Just after his thirty-ninth birthday, in early December, my anger cooled off and I reached out beyond texting. He answered my call sitting at the side of the road in the Hollywood Hills in tears. He and the Mountain were over. After that, the patterns I'd come to expect from him became more unpredictable and moved faster.

The last time I'd physically seen David, he had been leaving my apartment to catch an early morning plane to Los Angeles.

Nine months later, after the Mountain, multiple moves, and a car accident, David looked unwell, his face sunken, his smile strained. When I'd hugged him at the SFO arrivals gate, I felt his ribs and shoulder blades where muscle, the climbing holds of his flesh and desire, used to be. Cradling someone's body, feeling their pulse, the warmth of their breath on your neck, immediately corrects any mirage created, compressed, and transmitted over digital devices.

"You can't hide this from me," I said. "I see you."

David's lip trembled, and he let loose his sadness. "I can't hide this from you."

Yes, he can.

Sitting with David in Oakland, I was managing my own experience hour by hour; this was progress from clocking the milliseconds of survival. Over the winter I found a cycle that kept me moving forward. If I wasn't in bed sleeping, I was in therapy. If I wasn't in therapy, I was praying to asparagus. If I wasn't praying, I was practicing in a yoga class. If I wasn't in a yoga class, I was in conversation with David. If I wasn't in conversation with David, I was sleeping. Every day at five thirty-eight I would face west and feel the daylight hours growing longer. I would feel the warmth of the sun on my skin contrast with the cold air flowing in and out of my lungs. I'd think of the Danish words inscribed on a copper and marble sundial — inherited from my great-grandmother — that read, "Do as I, count only the bright hours." Then the cycle would restart. When David had turned his attention back to me, I was living second by second. David could sit in the rawness of my experience and I could sit in his. Over the winter, we became lifelines for each other. We coached and created a profound system of mutual support. We had some of the most in-depth and complex conversations of my life about god, death, and childhood trauma. I labeled these dense dialogues "Exercises in Advanced Human-ing."

I related to how his heartbreak expressed itself — the burning in the chest and wrists, the loss of appetite, the sobriety of feeling everything — because those were my body's reactions after he'd left me. I encouraged David to flip into Beyoncé mode: buy a freakum dress, take a bat to a fire hydrant, and *get in formation*. But what churned in him was an obsession about the Mountain that sparked erratic behavior. One day David was in Baha, Mexico, and the next he was leaving LA and moving back to San Francisco. Two hours later he signed an apartment lease in Oakland, ten minutes after that he was careening up the shoulder of Interstate 5 with all his worldly possessions packed in a Honda Fit. Four seconds later, a tractor trailer had ripped the door off his car and David was on his way to the hospital. Three hours later he was reconnecting with his birth father while buying a used couch off the internet. I felt enmeshed with his nervous system, feeling his extreme highs and low lows.

By the time I landed in San Francisco, David hadn't slept more than a few hours a night in a few weeks. Emotional distress during a recent therapy session had triggered a psychogenic seizure that quaked his body. He began to write day and night, but the writing he shared with me was emotionally dense, unclear. I grew more concerned for his welfare but couldn't accurately gauge his experience through the devastation of my own, from the physical distance that separated us. I had no baseline for reasonable emotional reactions, other than unease in my stomach. I believed David was manic because I felt turbulent alongside him, and although it felt wrong to measure my experience against his, I needed to tell him what I was perceiving.

"I'm not pathologizing you. I'm asking you to identify your experience. To put a word to your feelings so that I know how to care for you."

David stared off towards the bandstand, he took a shallow breath, and his bottom lip grew tight. As the tension gathered in his face and chest, I braced myself for a very public argument. But instead of deflecting or lashing out, he paused and relaxed. I saw clarity on his face, and his energy calmed.

"*Fuck*, you're right. None of this is real. I need to call Loren."

David got up from where we sat, and he walked along the promenade on his phone. He disappeared out of sight behind the twisted and gnarled New Zealand tea trees planted by the edge of the water. Sculpted by the wind, the trees formed surrealist arches coiling out of the earth and melting down with braided ropes of branches and deeply fluted thick trunks. I felt like one of these crooked trees.

"Loren says that I'm bipolar," David said, plunking himself down on the grass. "I guess I forgot."

David was not bipolar, and this was not what Loren said, but you don't know that.

"You forgot you are bipolar?"

"I'm not bipolar. I'm on the spectrum. I have high highs and low lows. I guess."

"Okay, we're going to the hospital."

"No. I don't want to go to the hospital."

Loren was on the other side of that phone call begging David to get to the hospital, but you also don't know that.

"Why's that?"

"I don't have insurance." He shrugged. "I missed the November buy-in. I'm getting bridge insurance on Monday."

"I don't care about money," I said. "I'll put it on my credit card."

"Is it okay if we skip the movie?" he said, growing agitated. "I just want to go home."

"Let's go home, but we're doing research and making a plan," I said.

There already was a long-standing protocol and plan of action, but you also don't know that.

David had found an affordable apartment and moved to Temescal, a rapidly gentrifying neighborhood in Oakland ten minutes from Lake Merritt and the picturesque downtown. Driving in the car with David was where I caught my more obnoxious behavior as I continually commented on the garbage-strewn streets. I kept a running count of the encampments set up by the homeless. I righteously judged the city as if I came from a pristine place without inequality or negligence. It was the contrast of extremes that chilled me: lean-tos, tarps, and shopping carts against well-kept properties with SUVs and Jurassic-sized succulents. With my elbow propped on the window ledge and my two fingers dug into the top seal of the car window, I caught David looking at my wrist. He read Matt's nickname, Elby, tattooed in fine line letters.

"Did it hurt?"

"Just cat scratches."

"I don't know how you're doing it."

"Remember what you said to me before I flew here?"

"Trust your life."

"Trust your life," I repeated back.

"I did say that." He smirked.

"You have many slogans, David Martinez; you should quote yourself more often."

Our emotions were at the surface of every word, and only a thin membrane separated us from tears. We heated then dissipated, and as we cooled, we coagulated. We formed a temporary film, a pot of cream of tomato soup resting on a stovetop. Our conversation was a delicate reckoning, expressions of sorrow balanced with laughter. It felt good to make David laugh, to breathe levity into his discomfort. It felt wonderful to have a companion in sadness who wasn't a cat or a therapist.

"I should have been there for you," David said.

"Yup, you did fuck off. You should have flown to Toronto. I needed you."

"I know," he conceded in a rare moment. "It was too much."

"It was too much for *you*?" I laughed.

"I fucked things up between us."

"No, you didn't. I mean . . . you didn't make it easy," I corrected. "But I'm still here in the seat beside you."

I placed my left hand on his thigh and smiled lovingly at David as tears flooded his eyes. "I still love you, but I need you to know that once I move to California, I'm going to spend all my spare time collecting litter off the road and not with you."

"Shawn!" David shook his head, rolling his eyes, trying not to laugh before cracking into giggles. "I'll get you a wide-brimmed garbage sunhat."

"I'll look so sexy in my garbage sunhat."

Ruby Street was a typical residential street lined with Honda Fits. David's building was four-story stucco walk-up with large lead-pane bay windows, scalloped moldings, and modern Victorian peaks. A gray fire escape zippered the frontage. David's unit was on the second floor to the left, facing the street. From the sidewalk, I could see a copper vase of fresh alstroemerias purchased from Trader Joe's sitting on David's altar in the bay window. We entered the coved lobby, and David collected a stack of envelopes bound with elastics from his mailbox. As we climbed a wide wooden staircase, I ran my hand along the white stucco walls, thinking there was a luxury building underneath layers of paint and cheap upgrades.

David had crafted a peaceful and minimalist home. Everything was in a soft white or gray palette, which allowed for beautiful pieces like a crimson and navy blue Persian rug to define the space. Some of it was familiar to me from the Sex-Positive Home; other pieces were revealed from the storage lockers David finally emptied. I eased off my shoes, and a stream of sand collected from the morning hike trickled to the floor. The heels and soles of my socks were soaked in blood, the inside of my shoes painted maroon. I slowly peeled off my socks; my bare feet smelled of ammonia and iron. I tiptoed to the kitchen garbage to toss my socks into the trash. I watched David standing by the kitchen sink, opening the stack of letters, one by one. He'd rip, unfold a page, read, then sigh. Each letter was a rejection from his previous insurance company, every blue and white page denying a medical claim, thousands of dollars of nos. David slumped over in disappointment.

I walked over and held him from behind.

"It's gonna be okay," I said.

"Shawn," David said, looking down at the floor. "You're bleeding all over my floor."

We both lost it, laughing hysterically.

As night approached, David began researching insurance companies. He also negotiated a generous part-time contract with a tech company that would secure his next three months' income. He found three clinics in San Francisco where he could obtain Seroquel, an antipsychotic drug that restores the balance of neurotransmitters, plus mental health support groups for gay men. I watched him work like an air-traffic controller. Over hipster hamburgers at a Temescal bar, we developed a protocol and a strategy for the next few weeks: exercise, regular meals, drinking water. David would exchange a set of keys with a new friend he planned on going to Tahoe with in the upcoming weeks. There were hiccups in the flow as he flipped in and out of Beyoncé mode, and I switched in and out of grief. Then we curled up on the couch together like lovers and watched a movie. We said good night, and David went to his bedroom while I shut the door to the living room and slept on an air mattress — this was the closest to dating in the same city we got. My back slumped into the bed, and I thought about the end of vigorous yoga practice and savasana as the reward from efforting and exhausting oneself. I thought about yoga as a practice of throwing everything up in the air and seeing how it lands. I thought of the separation between David and me. And, as I closed my eyes, I longed to be next to him.

On Sunday morning, I made scrambled-egg burritos and coffee while Joni Mitchell's *Miles of Aisles* played lightly on the speaker in the living room. David had let me sleep in while he fielded phone call after phone call: responses to long personal emails that he had crafted all night instead of sleeping. While I had rested, he had whipped himself into frenetic energy, working through most of his contact list by sunrise. David ghosted in and out of the apartment, talking in private on the sidewalk outside, as his contacts woke up across time zones and called him after reading his cryptic emails. After he finished a long phone call with his father, I handed him a plate of food and ordered him to sit down and eat. "You haven't slept, and you need food," I mothered. I sat and watched him eat. He lit up. He didn't scarf it down but savored in silence. He took deep breaths between bites, his chest expanded, and his shoulders dropped. He pointed to the last bites of burrito in his hand, smiled, and gave an approving thumbs-up.

"Who is this singing?" David asked, listening to the lyrics of "Cactus Tree."

"David, it's Joni Mitchell."

"Oh yeah, I forgot," he said. "I like her."

"You forgot who Joni Mitchell is?"

His phone rang, and David exited the apartment. From the window I watched him pacing back and forth in the street, unsure of what I was looking at or for. David was an advanced algebra question I didn't feel smart enough to solve. He had therapists and practitioners he worked with. Nobody in his immediate community was flagging his behavior as worrisome. His house was neat and orderly. He was making plans weeks in advance, committing to new work; he bought deodorant and guest sheets at Target on our way home from the airport. The facts did not match the abstractions I was privy to, and I credited the disparity to my shortcomings. I was the irritant, and the further away I was, the more stable he was. I woke up feeling like an inconvenience to David, an unwanted guest, the obstacle in his day. We had already canceled plans to drive over the bridge for a morning service at Glide Memorial; the day was quickly slipping away, and my flight back to LA was early Monday morning. So, I did the dishes, deflated the mattress, showered, and moved forward. The next time David entered the apartment, I stopped him in the hallway.

"I'm going to the farmers market around the corner to look at the produce, then afterwards I'd like to go to Bernal Heights."

"I don't know if that's a good idea."

"I'm not leaving San Francisco until you tell Rachael in person what's going on with you," I said. "Get showered. You're better with fresh air."

Visiting the farmers market was about me, so was the stop at a Mexican gift shop in the Mission where I bought a generic howlite calavera, but taking David to see Rachael in Bernal Heights was about David. Bernal Heights meant safety and it meant synchronization. We parked the car at the foot of the steep hill outside the Boise Street home. David grew nervous, and he asked to hold my orange rock skull as we climbed the staircase. He squeezed it in his palm before slipping it in his front pocket. The front door opened before we could knock. I remembered how Rachael and John welcomed guests into their home with an actual open-door policy. There were hugs and pleasantries, and a few jokes about my inevitable return to Bernal Heights as cheer briefly erased the disaster of my last five months. John and I started cracking puns, and I thanked Rachael for the taco socks she'd gifted me for my birthday. We left John to continue reading the newspaper cover to cover, and the three of us began the circling walk up to the summit.

Spring covered the rock mound with lush greenery, and a gentle wind blew through the young grass with a silver shimmer. The rock and dirt cracked under our feet as we paced the slow incline. I grew proud of David as he quickly initiated a deeper conversation, cutting past the work chitchat, and how easily Rachael waded into nurture. Their relationship was unique, grafted of many archetypes: they spliced together the roots and scions of their best qualities — it felt copasetic and vital. As David spoke, Rachael offered a loving pat on the back, and when the conversation got sticky, she shared a story from her recent vacation in Italy or a fact about the neighborhood. David was incredibly soft as he spoke. The Stranger had long been eviscerated in the heat of heartbreak. I found myself relieved that he was expressing himself in person and not over email or text. The pot had been taken off the stove.

We crested the hill and settled around the area where David and I had spotted the coyote a year earlier, where we'd impetuously agreed that we were a yes for each other. We plucked at the grass shoots, letting the mid-afternoon sun fall on our faces for half an hour. We talked with ease.

"Well, you two have had quite the year," said Rachael.

"You know in old cartoons where a pilot is landing a plane, but it falls apart as it hits the runway? The plane lands, but the pilot is holding only the control wheel?" I waxed. "That's what this year feels like . . . peeled away but still holding the wheel."

Rachael laughed, and David looked over the basin of the city.

"David, honey," Rachael offered. "It's all going to be okay. This is nothing we haven't tackled before."

Rachael understood his history, had witnessed his seizures, and been in the emergency room with him before. David looked at her. He smiled. I smiled, too, thinking about how many times in my life, in my most dire moments, I had yearned for that type of assurance and care from a parental figure.

I took my first breath in San Francisco.

I helped Rachael walk down the steepest part of the slope while David trudged ahead. We said our goodbyes outside the car, and my parting with Rachael felt permanent, like this was my last trip to Bernal. As we drove down Alabama, past the Sex-Positive

Home, away from Boise, David freed his sadness. He chugged back his tears and his jaw quaked uncontrollably.

"David," I said. "Love, what is going on? Pull over."

"No." His lips trembled with his words. "I need to keep moving."

"Okay. We'll keep moving," I said. "But I'm going to touch you."

I unbuckled my seat belt, squared my body towards him and placed my right hand on his breastbone while sliding my left hand between his shoulder blades. I held him like this and prompted him to focus on his breath. David was not going to stop moving; he was determined to get somewhere. It wasn't the same energy he'd had while driving up the shoulder of the interstate. I knew this because I'd been on the phone with him, telling him to pull over, to stop, when the accident happened. I didn't know what this was. I was frightened as we drove over the Bay Bridge in silence, crossing the long curved expanse above treacherous water. I feared that he'd somehow cause an accident that launched the car into the air. I could imagine the view as the windshield tipped down to blue water, and my organs rose to my throat as my feet pressed steady against the floor. I did not fear death. I feared the absurdity death brings.

"Just breathe, Shew," I coached as we reached the midway point and tunneled our way through Yerba Buena Island and came out the other side. "Just breathe."

David's energy dissipated as the car rolled into Oakland. He pulled into the nearest gas station to pick up a pack of cigarettes. David had gone the entire weekend without smoking, and I was relieved to watch him smoke his American Spirits on the pavement outside the apartment. I started to pack and plot my next week in LA. My exhaustion came to the forefront as David entered sometime after dark.

"I was outside talking on the phone," he half-apologized.

I responded with silence as I grabbed my ruined sneakers in the foyer.

"I guess this wasn't the weekend we planned, was it?"

"David, I'm here." I turned. "Please tell me you see me."

"I see you."

"Good, because one year ago we stood on Ocean Beach and you told me I wasn't here, that I wasn't present, and you were right. I was trapped in the past. But I've walked through fucking hell with you and away from you, and I'm finally standing here with you. I'm here."

"I know."

"So, where the fuck is everyone else? Why do I feel abandoned with you? Where is the Forest? Where is the Mountain? Where are all the men from the fucking bathhouse?"

"Shawn . . ."

"No, this whole weekend you've acted disappointed that it's me who showed up for you and not someone else."

"Shawn, you're getting worked up. You're irrational."

"I'm not irrational. I'm impaired. I am broken. Do you understand? Half of me died with Matt. I feel dead, and I'm confused — like I'm being gaslit. Something isn't right and whatever this is . . ."

"I know."

"I'm the one who is standing here. After all the shit you've put us through, I still love you. I feel like the fucking joke, but I will feed you. I will bathe you. I will pay for whatever treatment. I will fly you to Canada and marry you so that you have healthcare."

"Shawn."

"I can't and I won't lose another man I love."

I became winded and collapsed in the foyer; David caught me and eased us onto the floor. He held me and kissed my forehead, and I wept onto his body. Then I held him as he cried. Couples, lovers, friends fight. We tear apart and we heal, scar tissue changing how we reattach. David and I were emulsified goo on the floor. We had no shape, no form, just messes — two scared boys on the floor waiting for the adults to show up.

> *Contained in the library of the body, hidden deep in the shelves, in one of the very first volumes is a little story. Written long ago but never forgotten, only faintly remembered as an echo, is a story of two boys who were so close in age, they could have been brothers. One hot summer day, while the elders gathered outside, the two boys found curiosity in each other's bodies. They hid in an upstairs bedroom, showing each other their wonders and comparing their universes, until an elder keeping watch came upon the young explorers in mid-discovery. The elder attacked the children. The two boys held on tight to each other. "Let go!" the elder demanded. Torn apart, the boys screamed towards one another. The younger boy was dragged down the stairs by the wrist. He felt the carpet burn on his skin, he smelled nicotine in the air, and collected salt tears in the back of his throat. Taken behind a shed, he learned to transform his back into a rock so he did not feel the lashes past the first few.*

The elders formed a council, for they feared the nature of the rock child. The two boys were separated forever, and the slightly older boy grew to dislike the younger boy. The rock boy became funny and used his shield to deflect both pain and pleasure. He did not feel his body as he grew to be an adult. Still, he felt the scorching heat of a dry summer in his wrists and chest every time he was pulled from another man. He felt the sweltering intensity of July over and over until he heard the whisper and opened the volume containing this story. He remembered.

"You can stay one more night if you need to," David said, running his hand along my back and kissing my ear. His words cut.

Let go.

"I'm sorry, David. This isn't about me," I said. "I need to get back to LA and meet with my immigration lawyer so I can eventually be here for you. Even if I end up just being your goddamn neighbor."

I eased myself off the floor and continued to pack in the living room. David rose and held me from behind. He placed the orange skull into my palm and kissed the back of my neck.

"Don't forget," he said, closing my palm around the rock.

I was already awake when David knocked on the living room door shortly after six thirty in the morning.

"Can I walk you to the subway?" he asked.

"That would be great," I said, rolling off the air mattress.

I brushed my teeth and threw on some travel clothes, and we left the apartment. MacArthur Station was a short fifteen-minute walk from Ruby Street. The morning air was crisp, and as we neared the BART station, daylight broke. David and I held hands, not talking, the sound of my duffel bag thwacking against my leg. David was calm. He was present. We took our time relishing the last moments of our weekend together in silence. As we stepped over a trash bag that had ripped open, its contents strewn all over the sidewalk, David gave me a look, as if asking me to not spoil the moment with my anti-litter talking points. I laughed.

The entrance to MacArthur Station was under a highway overpass. When we reached the blue gates, David handed me his Clipper card from his leather wallet.

"Here, use this." He placed it in my hands. "Mail it back to me when you get to LA."

"David!" I was surprised. "Are you sure?"

"Yup."

"I'll give you a call when I get settled in Los Feliz. Okay?"

"Sounds good."

I heard the BART train screeching into the station. I didn't want to rush the goodbye so I opted to let it pass and wait for the next train. David wrapped his left hand around the small of my back and pulled me into his body. Our groins connected. Our foreheads rested together, and our lips joined. His right hand pressed on my left ribs. I felt him warming me through thin layers of fabric. I felt a wave of aliveness in my body, a surge of magnetism between us. We kissed long and passionately. It was the first time in the whole weekend that our desire surfaced.

"I love you. I've always loved you," David said.

"I love you too," I repeated back. "I'm still a yes for us."

"I'm a yes for you."

"Let's get through this, and we can talk about partnership again, okay?"

"I'd like that." He smiled.

"This is where partnership begins for me," I said.

We kissed until I heard the next train in the distance. It was the most passionate kiss of my life.

"I gotta go." I pulled away.

"Okay."

"Remember I'm only an hour flight away. Love you, Shew."

I tapped the card and walked through the gates. David waved, turned, and walked back towards his apartment. I got on the subway and left for Los Angeles.

I would replay these last choices over and over in the months ahead.

Luck is a word that I use very carefully.

Some might consider me an unlucky person, but I believe luck shines on me generously. To me, luck is surviving an unexpected twist of fate.

In hindsight, I feel incredibly lucky that I was in Los Angeles when I learned David completed suicide just hours after we had parted ways at MacArthur Station.

LA was built with room for dreams to shatter — with its low architecture and tar pits, it's only a short descent for the city's angels to fall. My luck was that a city characterized by vapidity, fame, and glamor responded to my crisis. My luck was seeing the precious humanity in LA, as I explored it through a lens of loss and not ambition.

Luck was the generosity of Gemma, Rachael and John's daughter, in the moments after learning about David. "Come over," she texted. "It's safe here." I grabbed an overnight bag and hailed a rideshare to east LA, where Gemma was waiting for me on her Highland Park porch step.

"Did I kill David?" I asked her.

"No." She soothed me with an embrace. "Come in. I've just boiled some water for tea."

Luck was the springtime superbloom that released an ungodly amount of pollen — for me, a natural tranquilizer that caused almost narcoleptic powerdowns. Luck was coming to under a palm without a sunburn. Luck was the actor friends and film festival buddies who came out of the hills to host dinners, who refilled my wineglass, who encouraged me to hold their children and pet their animals, who tracked me as I walked the unwalkable city, openly sobbing on its hiking trails and confirming my whereabouts by taking and sending griefies at scenic canyon peaks. My luck was the strangers who looked at me with empathy, as if they, too, had lost a beloved development deal or failed to book that breakout part.

Luck was the phone call from Rachael asking me to return to San Francisco at the end of the week. It was seeing a Día de los Muertos enamel pin on the table of a street vendor outside Grauman's Chinese Theatre, just when I needed a sign, needed to find enough meaning to choose not to retreat to Canada. It symbolized my decision to stay, to not bypass the pain of what was ahead. Luck was connecting with a compassionate customer service agent at United Airlines who waived the cost of a round-trip flight to San Francisco and who offered to pray for me as I broke down in tears.

I try not to dwell on the path not taken, but as I looked out the window on the tarmac of the Hollywood Burbank Airport at the ground speeding faster and faster, I recognized this moment as the point of no return in my life.

What if is a dangerous question. Because it did not happen, I can gently speculate on the *what if* I had closed myself off and returned to Toronto, bypassing David's death. With the despair I carried for Matt, the state of my nervous system, my age, sexuality, familial support, I know with more certainty than I'd care to possess that David's suicide would have been my ultimate unraveling. I stood on that precipice: one slip from deep isolation, spiraling into nothingness, pleading with a cloaked specter to tell me the name of the deceased engraved on stone, refusing to look upon the name until forced to read my own. Because it did not happen, I wake up every day, alive, excited for my first cup of coffee.

Only now with two feet firmly planted on this earth can I see how it could have gone all wrong — but didn't.

That is luck.

April 6, 2019

David was San Francisco; San Francisco was David. I didn't know this city without him.

I heard him guiding me towards Rachael and John's home as I exited the 24th Street Mission Station and headed west towards Philz Coffee. I clutched my orange howlite skull with my left hand as my right hand fiddled with the pin now affixed to my gray hoodie above the burning hot sensation on my ribs. My lips tingled.

I walked with confidence while in conversation with David. I saw Guadalajara, the burrito place. "Your face lit up tasting horchata for the first time," he said. I passed the independent bookstore where a dog always nests in the handlebar basket of a bicycle. David warned me off as I looked through a Mexican bakery window: "It looks good, but it's like chewing on sawdust." I saw the chairs outside Philz where we sat early in the morning, sharing a cinnamon bun. I turned south towards Bernal Heights. "Remember, Cesar Chavez Street divides Bernal Heights from the Mission," he instructed. I crossed the wide thoroughfare and continued uphill before cutting through Precita Park. "This is perfect!" he whispered from under our tree. I saw the minibus painted like an American flag outside the Precita Park Cafe. I saw David having his morning breakfast sandwich (or three) before turning to walk up Alabama. I looked at the peak of what used to be David's room in the Sex-Positive Home. "That was the balcony where you held me after we first had sex on PrEP," I told him. "You were so nervous," he said. "Well, I trusted you, but I was also scared." I shrugged. David leaned down to pat Ziggy, the old black cat who roamed the northeast corner of Bernal. "You do have unique relationships with animals," I said. We turned onto Boise, and after a short but steep incline, we arrived at the foot of Rachael and John's terrazzo staircase. "Here, David." I passed him the dahlia plant we'd purchased from a Pescadero farm. "You hand it to Rachael."

I saw movement from the kitchen table inside. The yellow front door opened, and Loren walked out wearing a white linen button-down, light blue jeans. Behind David's eyeglasses refitted with blank lenses, her dark eyes sparkled through her shock. Loren stood with the compact strength of a dancer and ran a hand through her short raven hair. We looked at each other and took deep breaths. *You were invited to Loren's wedding, but you didn't end up attending. I mean, you were there but virtually. You listened to David read the poem he marked in a collection of poetry before he offered it to Loren and her husband as a gift. You received an onslaught of photos from the reception when David ripped the seat out of his pants. The pants you sewed for him. David tried to blame your workmanship, but he got an extra three months' wear. How did you and Loren not have each other's telephone numbers?*

~··~

I knew. It had started as a quiet doubt as I landed at LAX, as I looked at David's Clipper card in my wallet. It gained tension as David's texts became more sporadic, louder and louder as David stopped texting me altogether and as my calls went direct to his voicemail. Flashing lights when Loren first contacted me through my website and asked me to call her. A full and resonant train whistle, even though I convinced myself that everything was okay and went to watch Kathy Griffin perform a test set at the Laugh Factory while texting with Loren throughout for updates. Deafening as Loren tried to activate his people in San Francisco.

I was in my Airbnb in Los Feliz when I got the text from Loren shortly before midnight. "Shawn. I'm sorry. He's gone." Loren's message was exact; I remembered sending Matt's sister a similar message immediately after his passing. For hours, I had felt helpless, but with a single text I was dropped into the experience. I imagined the Ruby Street apartment: the flashing blue and red lights through the window, the first responders standing in and outside the apartment doorway, the yellow tape being unrolled, the curious neighbors peering out of their doorways.

"Fuck you, God," I blared. "*Fuck* you!"

I emptied out my remaining trust in the world. My ears pulsed, my jaw locked, volts of electricity shot from my hand to the base of my skull. My body convulsed.

I made my way to the bed, and I stared up at the exposed beams of the guesthouse ceiling and knew I was no longer safe inside myself. I quickly launched an emergency plan I'd crafted before traveling, a just-in-case-something-happens-but-don't-worry-Shawn-nothing-is-going-to-happen plan. The late-night calls went out across time zones to my pillars who would be woken up to bear this weight, to witness, to hear a man plead, "How is this happening again? I just wanted a vacation." There would be no reprieve or relief; there would be no vacation from the storm.

David's sibling, Tiff, followed Loren out of Rachael and John's wearing David's denim jacket. It was oversized on their small frame, but they wore it with an air of determination to grow and one day fill it. Tiff looked so like David it was too much, and I did a double take as I walked up the stairs.

"Hi, I'm Shawn," I said with a wave.

The realms of time and space we forged with David were colliding. I knew these two people profoundly in my mind but not in the flesh of their being. Metaphysical past lives? Romantic déjà vu? No. We were simply IRL-ing, and the by-product was an intense sense of familiarity without intimacy, knowledge mediated by David. Our relationships had run parallel to each other until a seismic event rerouted us: I saw Loren; I saw Tiff. Loren saw me; Tiff saw me. As I embraced them for the first time, I smelled David's cologne, and the hug felt like a mutual wringing of tears from each other. Our grief would be the intimacy that flooded, thickened, and bound us.

Rachael appeared in the doorway. I knew the look in her eyes, and my heart sank — it was the same look Louisa wore.

I found my people, and it felt so fucking weird and sad and joyous.

Loren, Tiff, and I packed into David's Honda Fit and traveled to his apartment in Oakland. After several mugs of espresso and warm milk and a large bowl of Rachael's homemade granola (the only nutrients I'd kept down other than the multi-scoop flights of ice cream from Jeni's in Los Feliz), I felt adequately fueled for this challenge. Loren and Tiff had been in the thick of discovery of David's life, sorting through his stuff and boxing it for the last few days. They had a playful sense of the enormously difficult task, a task that I was all too familiar with.

"You'll be surprised at how calming and soothing it is to be in the space." Loren offered me a reassuring look through David's frames. "We even slept over a couple of nights."

I looked over from the passenger seat and smiled.

"We're going to do a ritual for David tomorrow night," she added. "To send him extra energy on his journey."

Ritual?

"Hmm, when you say *ritual* . . ." I half asked. "I only know the word from when Matt died. Or when the Orangemen crashed my grandpa's funeral and started chanting 'our brother this,' 'our leader that,' and my sister and I just looked at each other thinking, *Holy fuck, Grandpa was a leader of the Orangemen?*"

"Wait!" Loren interrupted. "Your grandpa was an orange man? What does that even mean?"

"It means he hated Catholics and donated computers to public schools." I laughed. "Back to ritual?"

"I don't know. Ritual is something that has been a part of my own healing practice. It's what gets me through every challenge life throws at me. I just feel like we need to do this for David."

"I'd like to be there."

"Of course you must."

We listened to a Spotify playlist of David's music, his curated soundtrack of his life, as we crawled through Saturday afternoon San Francisco traffic. Held at a stoplight, I looked out beyond a barbed-wire fence and saw a street mural of a fallen Statue of Liberty. She is toppled, ripped from her plinth, and bound in chains. Her tabula ansata remains clutched to her person. Her torchbearing hand lies lifelessly at her side, yet the torch she once carried remains lit while suspended in the air, hovering over the words of Emma Lazarus's "New Colossus": *Give me your tired, your poor, Your huddled masses yearning to breathe free*. I pressed my back into the passenger seat and held it there as we crossed the Bay Bridge, into Oakland. I placed my palm on the nubs of bones between my clavicles and coached myself to breathe.

As we walked from the parked car on Ruby Street, I saw the bottom sash window of David's second-floor apartment was left open. The window was situated directly above an open garage bay packed with small industrial trash bins. I plotted my should've-would've strategy. I envisioned myself rolling the dumpsters out, climbing on top, breaking the screen, and pulling myself through the front window. I would have circumvented the property manager, who had waited for the police to arrive before taking action.

I felt a patch of heat flare on my left ribs.

"Don't think about it," Loren interrupted. "I know what you're doing. I would have done the exact same thing."

We entered the front door, collected David's mail, and walked up the wooden staircase, my hand again reading the high gloss stucco walls as we climbed. Loren turned the key and entered the apartment with Tiff. I paused behind them and readied myself to make the transition.

I stepped in the front door and began a meditative walk around the apartment. I breathed with each step. I observed fine details as if they would reveal a clue; as if there was a case to solve and I was the sleuth to crack it. Loren and Tiff resumed sorting in silence. The apartment looked disemboweled. David's possessions poured out of the closets and drawers onto the floor. But oddly the markers of my visit a week ago were unmoved, paused amongst the chaos of his stuff.

There was David Whyte's poem "The House of Belonging" hung on the wall and the deflated air mattress folded in the corner on the landing. The alstroemerias from Trader Joe's remained fresh in the copper vase on his altar; the throw pillow on the couch was still off-kilter from when I'd clutched it during a frail emotional moment. I turned into the kitchen. The loaf of bread from the farmers market was still in its bag on the IKEA dining table, my bloodied socks from the hike in Tilden were at the top of the trash, the pan I used to make omelets dried by the sink, and fanned on the counter were David's rejected insurance claims. I circled back into the foyer and down the hallway, allowing my hand to brush along the wall with one long continuous stroke, the wood floor creaking under my feet. In the bathroom sat his brand-new stick of deodorant. *Who buys deodorant two days before killing themself?* I stepped in the center of his bedroom and began a full-circle scan. He had no tchotchkes or mementoes in the bedroom. His mattress had been moved to the living room to accommodate Loren and Tiff's overnights. His closet door was open, a suit bag remained hanging on the rail, and the rest of his clothing was folded neatly in a blue IKEA bag. I trailed the baseboards around until I stopped at the doorway. I saw the white cloud-like paint chips sloughed onto the hardwood from the doorjamb. They had been shredded off from force — my mind flashed to the smear of Matt's blood on the hospital floor.

I assembled a peripheral understanding, a sketch of how David died. I felt the image.

I sank to the floor, leaned over the paint chips, and moaned. The movement in the living room came to a halt as Loren and Tiff held silent space for me to purge the sadness that snaked around my bowels and erupted from my mouth. I steadied myself by digging the pads of my palms and fingers into the hardwood. I began to pray silently. *I thank this apartment, and this now-hallowed room, for the dignity and shelter and privacy it provided my beloved in his most sacred moment.* Tears fell and pooled on the floor as I gently shrugged my shoulders like in a downward dog. *Thank you for the meals he ate, the words he wrote, the dreams he planned, the company he kept, the showers he took, the rest he earned, the pleasure he found within these confines.* I dug deeper into the knots of the wood, trying to knead and stretch it like clay. I thanked the skeleton of wood, the nervous system of wiring, the ventricles of plumbing, the skin of plaster that protected, provided, and lived with him the last weeks, days, hours, minutes, and seconds of his life. I breathed. *David died in his home, a sanctuary of his creation. For this, I am grateful.*

My stomach heaved up the remains of my prayer and rested.

"Shawn," Loren called after a long silence, "I'm thinking about making coffee for us. How does that sound?"

"I think that sounds great." I loosened my grip on the hardwood floor.

As twilight approached Sunday night, we started to shift from
packing, sorting, and preserving the stuff of David to the ritual.
It had been an emotional weekend, and we'd moderated our work
with oceanside walks, contemplative hikes up Bernal, and endless
cups of coffee. Along the way, we collected items for the ritual,
and we asked each other the difficult questions, the how and whys.
We braided our knowledge together, constructing timelines and
theories while deconstructing David's physical life. The absurdity of cleaning out another lover's apartment within five months
wasn't lost on Loren.

"How are you doing this again?" Loren asked.

"We just do it for our loves," I quoted Louisa.

"We just do it for our loves."

"Exactly."

She smiled. "I found something for you."

"Me?"

"Open your hand."

I unfurled my fingers and Loren dropped a smoke gray marble
in the basin of my palm. It was the bubble I had purchased for
David in a general store in Pescadero in exchange for the blue one
he gifted me.

He kept the bubble. I placed it safely in my pocket with the
orange skull.

We wrapped up by assigning some of David's things to
members of his community. We'd pick up an object and ask, Who

do we think would like this vase, sweater, book, rock, or framed picture? We were emotionally settling his estate. When items couldn't be stored, donated, or reused, the profoundly private objects entrusted with us to keep discreet, we took a black marker and wrote "We Love You" across their surfaces. We cleansed everything with palo santo smoke before bagging and placing it all in the dumpsters below. Tiff and Loren had multiple suit-cases to travel home. My pile was small: a copy of Kahlil Gibran's *The Prophet*, a blue scarf doused with his cologne, a green wool cardigan, and the bubble.

David's longtime friend Maureen arrived for the ritual. The buzzer rang, and Teresa joined us in the apartment. Teresa was a newer friend of David's. Both were the first to respond to Loren's texts. Teresa waited outside the apartment door for hours until the police arrived and the property manager would finally unlock the door. *I told David to give Teresa a key. Why didn't he?* I admired Teresa's tenacity, her ability to stay through difficult situations; she showed up for David in his most sacred moment.

"Do you imagine yourself braising a lot of meat or cooking stews?" I asked Teresa, holding up a Dutch oven.

"Umm, sure."

"Here, Teresa." I passed her the heavy cast iron. "Have a Le Creuset. Make your loved ones delicious meals and think of David."

With Loren leading us, we cleared a space on the Persian rug and set up before the sun went down. Using a compass, we aligned the dominant geometric points carved in a wooden mandala plate so that it faced north-south. The mandala acted as a grid, and Loren unwrapped a giant bluish-gray crystal from a hand towel and anchored it in the center. Tiff lit candles with David's lighter.

Maureen and Teresa set up the offerings: bowls of water (to slake the thirst of visiting spirits), salt (for purification), a Meyer lemon picked from Rachael's garden (for clarity and friendship), a bowl of Rachael's granola (food for passage). We incorporated the Trader Joe's alstroemerias and a single straw-yellow ice plant bloom picked from the berm of Ocean Beach. I lit a stick of palo santo then dusted the space with David's cologne while Loren turned on David's playlist.

We turned towards each other and formed a coven around an altar. The sun began to set. It was not light; it was not dark. It was between times. The ritual began as we offered our talismans for the grid. I placed my orange howlite skull in front of me. It joined the ranks of a small red Buddha, a graphite stone, a piece of sea glass, and a silver tag engraved with Walt Whitman's words "I am large, I contain multitudes." There was no chanting, no tongues, or sacrifice: just poetry. Tiff read a passage written by a West Coast poet. The words in Tiff's voice were powerful and stirred the rawness of my system. I found myself overwhelmed hearing the natural timber and inflexion of David's voice through Tiff, the unmistakable shared marker of genetics. It was as if Tiff and David were reciting it in unison. Maureen placed her hand on my back to steady me as I grabbed the nearby towel and blew my nose into it quietly.

We sat in silence and began our inner conversations with David. This time was our siloed opportunity to internally express what we were unable or denied a chance to say in life, what can be spoken only in death. Our words overlapped, creating a spectral conversation, and while seated in this formation, I came to understand the act of praying in a group. Prayer happens when you slow the pace of your thoughts, the constant running chatter, enough for meaning to trickle down and be felt as poetry in the body. Prayer is the drip-drip of language that collects longings and requests in the bowl of the pelvis. Prayer is stillness and silence, harnessing your internal dialogue with intention, and amplifying its power while in the safety of others.

"This feels good," Loren said marking the end of the ritual.

We blew out the candles. Loren took the gray hand towel and wrapped the crystal in it. I apologized for the wetness. "There was a superbloom in Los Angeles."

"Are you kidding me? This is all part of the soup. We're going to lock that mucus in."

The prayer I spoke to David during the ritual transformed into a sacred text for me. Afterwards, I transcribed it into a note which was placed in David's casket and cremated with his body.

I ended my prayer with a request.

Find the light in room 708.

Jayne was a tarot teacher and an intuit. She lived in "Little Florida," a brutalist apartment building in Toronto's chichi Yorkville. It's a complex for wealthy senior citizens who do not snowbird to time-shares or trailers in the Sunshine State; it has a movie theater, liquor and grocery store, restaurants — everything you need to survive the winter without stepping outside.

When I accepted Jayne's invitation to meet, I was neither curious about my future nor did I want to communicate with spirits. I had one question. It was a query that no reverend, gay elder, or therapist could resolve. It wasn't the textbook question about the meaning of life or what happens when you die. I didn't need to be comforted by concepts of someone being in a better place or reincarnated. The answer I sought was specific.

"How did I know?" I asked Jayne.

For twenty dollars, a palm reader with a street table once told me to never stare at my left palm because my frayed but long lines formed a pentacle. She didn't tell me why, but she advised not to look at the star formation. I'm not superstitious. I think that a bird in the house means you left the window open. I've served enough tables in restaurants to know that a dropped knife doesn't mean a mysterious man is arriving, but that you're clumsy with a tight cutlery roll-up. (It is a tradition in storytelling to present yourself as a skeptic before confessing your metaphysical experience.) I still don't gaze at my left palm.

On the night of Matt's accident, an empty mug I was holding slipped and smashed on the floor. I slumped over the counter and breathed heavily through my nostrils. My first thought wasn't about the shards on the ground, but of Matt. I picked up my phone and started to text him, to see if he was okay, but then I stopped myself. I shut down the impulse, but a sense of dread grew overnight. When I got the news in the early morning, I received it with equal parts shock and confirmation.

I confess this to you not because I claim to have a power, but because if I told Matt this story, he'd have accepted it as fact. Matt labeled it "my witch" because he thought it was creepy.

"Your witch?" Jayne deliberated while lightly shuffling a tarot deck. "I've never heard it called that before. Interesting." She paused as she cut the deck. "Do you pray?"

"I do," I admitted.

"Do you pray to God?" She resumed shuffling.

"I pray to asparagus."

"Never heard that one." Jayne chuckled. "And what do you pray for?"

"I ask for wholeness and clarity."

"Did you pray before Matt died?"

"I did."

"What did you pray for?"

"For the strength to let him go."

"And?"

"My prayer was answered."

Jayne was the archetype of a grandma — sweet and unassuming. Her apartment was Wedgwood blue and laid out with heavy oak furnishings fit for a larger home. She had no personal photos, plants, or knickknacks. The dining table was covered in a thick sheet of clear protective plastic. There were no psychic symbols, crystals, beaded curtains, neon signs, or burning incense. There were no theatrics. I watched Jayne shuffle the cards like we were partners between hands of euchre, except it was never my turn to deal. She was exacting in her words, and she spoke with clarity that I dreamed of commanding. She said things only a Russian hacker would know about me, intimate details that raised the hair on my skin. We spoke with a teacher and student dynamic.

"What are the ways you shut yourself off?" she asked.

"Pardon?"

"The fact you ask this big question means you turn yourself off."

"I'm not sure I follow."

"When Matt's accident happened, what did you feel?"

"I felt him reach through my chest."

"When did you know David was dead?" Jayne paused in shuffling the deck. "Was it when you got the call?"

"No."

"Then when?"

"Hours before."

"When was that?"

"When he dropped the connection."

"Exactly. What did you feel?"

"I couldn't feel him; it's like he just disappeared and disconnected his phone."

In Ovid's telling of the Cëyx and Alcyone myth, Alcyone has two premonitions, gut feelings, that her husband will die at sea. She begs him first not to go, then after he insists on taking the dangerous journey across the Aegean Sea, she begs to travel and die with him. Cëyx denies her instinct and orders her to stay. While sailing to consult the oracle of Apollo, Cëyx's ship is overtaken by a violent storm, and he calls out his wife's name as he drowns in the churning black waters. As days pass, Alcyone continues to pray and prepare for her lover's safe return. Then Juno, the goddess of marriage, sends Morpheus, a master mimic, to tell Alcyone of her husband's demise. Morpheus appears in a dream as a drowned Cëyx. Morpheus, as her husband, begs her to abandon hope of his return. In the morning, Alcyone wakes in distress, knowing her love is dead. Moved by grief she runs to the sea shore and finds the body of Cëyx washing in on the horizon.

Alcyone's knowing is confirmed.

"How did you know?" Jayne asked.

"I just felt it."

"Exactly," she said. "So, how did you know?"

"I just knew."

May 29, 2019

In the flashbacks, I'm with David at MacArthur Station in Temescal. David hands me his Clipper card from his leather wallet. He pulls me in. We kiss, and my heart swells. Our foreheads rest together and our lips connect. I can feel his hand pressing on my left ribs and the other pressed against the small of my back. I feel him warming me through thin layers of fabric.

He says, "I love you. I've always loved you. I'm a yes for you."

"I'm still a yes for you. This is where partnership begins," I say. "I love you."

We kiss long and soft before breaking away from each other, and I turn my back and enter the subway station. I look back to see David walking away, his shoulders slightly rounded and deflated. I run after him; the turnstiles clunk open and closed. I call, "David." He stops. He smiles. I take his hand, and I never let go. We walk back to the apartment, and David isn't dead. David is alive because I never let go.

This was the rewrite my body created, the rewrite my fact-checking brain denounced. My body was begging for relief, but my brain was corrective and punitive. The body pled, "I need this comfort." The brain argued, "But that's not the truth. None of this is true. You left him. You walked away. You didn't chase after him. You killed David." The body screamed, "I told you something was wrong. I knew it. But you convinced me otherwise." The brain flexed its superiority saying, "I will make you suffer." I was suspended between the two, a child caught between incompatible and frustrated parents: one craving care and forgiveness, the other violently insisting on its need to be right.

The flashbacks are interruptive, overwhelming, and I lose a sense of time and space. I smell the tobacco notes of David's cologne. My left rib cage radiates heat, and my lips tingle. The spells grew more frequent and more intense as details and perspectives pieced together from conversations with others were connected. Information was chiropractic — it shifted and moved truth around and jammed against my own experience. This was the vital work of understanding the whys and the hows surrounding David's death, but my brain struggled to distinguish what it knew now from what it knew in the moment. And so, the clearer the picture became, the greater the punishment my brain delivered and the deeper I slipped into the past.

I became a time traveler.

Arriving back in San Francisco for David's memorial in May was like jumping right back into the action of an emotional cliff-hanger. As I stood at a microphone in front of an audience of David's community, I was silently pleading with the brain and body to make peace. I was worried about what would happen tomorrow when there was nothing left to coordinate or busy myself with and I was left to sit in my grief with no means to channel it.

David's "The Future Is Feeling" slogan was projected onto the black theater floor. A tribute video has successfully screened; the food, catered by the community, to the left of me looked bountiful and generous; and the floral arrangements by Teresa were beautiful. The print program was fresh off the press, as were the keepsake buttons with David's many catchphrases, the obituary I wrote ran with the photo I snapped at brunch a year earlier, and the ink trace of David's signature on the guestbook cover had dried. Everything — the tablecloths, the gels in lighting, the ribbons, the ink in the pens — matched a color palette gleaned from the hex codes embedded in David's professional website design. There were multiple spreadsheets, a budget, and weekly production meetings; this memorial had the workload of a professional theater show as I offered my full energy. The sad irony was not lost on me that a year earlier I had been preening and preparing my apartment to introduce David to my community, and now I was doing the same in part to introduce myself to his.

Stage right, I was supported by the members of what we took to calling the grief camp, the collective of friends and family members dealing with David's affairs. The individuals committed to showing up for their friend both in life and in death.

Before the ritual in Oakland, we'd all gathered that Sunday morning in a Noe Valley apartment. It was a '60s white-carpeted time capsule with a panoramic view of the basin. This was the space where my perceptions of David's distinct storylines collapsed as one by one his friends arrived, some bringing offerings of his favorite food, all carrying a fog of sheer disbelief. These were the friends whose borrowed cars I rode in, whose screengrabbed texts I read, and whose daily struggles I listened to through David, but I had never met. Names were assigned to faces and voices, shapes were drawn to bodies. Meeting each other felt as if we all had inadvertently studied each other over time. We were acquaintances ambiguously connected through the one man not in attendance. We all knew way more than we should of each other's lives. David didn't trade in gossip, though he wove the stories of those he loved into the forefront of his experience. He never breached our trust in life, and this value in death is what bonded the collective together.

Loren sat on the carpeted floor and started the gathering with absolute truth.

"Suicide was always an option," she said. "You need to understand with David suicide was always an option. It was never off the table."

My stomach dropped. The collective absorbed these words. Everything came into focus and my thinking cleared. Five minutes: I learned after clicking hyperlinks sent to me about suicide. Five minutes or less is the amount of time between ideation and action for someone to contemplate and impulsively end their own life.

David's last words were written in the tradition of Ho'oponopono, the Hawaiian practice of reconciliation and forgiveness. His handwriting conveyed an explosion of emotions, a storm of energy. My hands warmed when I held the paper. I read along with my fingertips. I remembered tracing the swirl of David's beard on his right cheek with the same finger and nicknaming him Hurricane Martinez.

The pot boiled over.

I looked out into the audience from the stage at the memorial, and I saw the Forest, the Mountain. I became immediately insecure in my relationship to David. Who was I in this situation other than the Canadian who carried a torch for a man whose memorial expenses now sat on a credit card, the would-be fiancé who held on through the Forest and the Mountain? *But then you turned your back and got on a subway?*

I felt David's hand pressed against my ribs, my lips tingled. David whispered, "Shawn, just let it be messy."

If I was the Boyfriend, then there must be a First Wife. I found him in the crowd: Damien, a tall, gorgeous, vibrant man sitting in the back with his twin sister. Although David's death complicated my mourning of Matt, it offered me a do-over, a way of practicing my new knowledge in a situation where the roles were reversed. It had felt imperative that Damien and I meet before the memorial. Bridging a connection with Damien wasn't an attempt to jumper-cable a deeper relationship with David; it was about practicing radical kindness and capacity, with the understanding that love is not a scarce resource that needs stockpiling. Mourning is like a piece of abstract art, and we must paint from as many angles as possible to include the whole experience of the deceased.

We met in a tea shop with chunky carved wooden furniture in the basement of a deconsecrated church in Hayes Valley. It was in a healing space with a yoga and meditation studio and free wi-fi for the freelancers in the adjacent Buddhist-themed workroom. Damien had chiseled features, black facial hair with salt-and-pepper edges, and various tattoos. He spoke with a soft California accent, and it was soothing to hear his experience of David without feeling the need to overwrite mine. Our conversation went multiple pots of Earl Grey longer than expected. There were many parallels as we compared relationship notes, and he graciously held my hand when I broke down over what color of ribbon I should use as a decor accent. We never know the inner dynamics of a couple's relationship, the ecology of two people, but I found myself growing frustrated with David. My direct experience of Damien was different from what David had shared with me, and this schism spoke more to David's suffering than his gripes of partnership. The only time I'd use the word *crazy* in association with David: he was nuts for breaking up with the man that sat beside me. And I wondered about the stories David told of me, to the community I now stood in front of.

I've never been out of place in front of a microphone. Nervous, yes. Not a right fit for the lineup, definitely. I wasn't there to deliver a moment or win over an audience. I wanted to be vulnerable in front of a community in mourning, but I didn't know if I could stop myself from letting out everything — the anger, the confusion. I didn't know how to begin, and I wanted to communicate with the conciseness of language that David demanded in conversation. I needed to be precise. I imagined myself as Blue Eyeliner.

"This is shit," I said.

I thought back to the mural of a fallen Statue of Liberty near the ramp to the Bay Bridge and when I'd sat on the edge of David's couch, clutching a pillow, unable to catch my breath. "I think this country is going to kill my spirit," I sobbed. I was overwhelmed and carried this ominous belief that nobody gave a shit if either David or I lived or died. We, too, were disposable. "This land is an embarrassment of riches, and this is what Americans do with it?" I declared through tears. David held me from behind, and he placed his lips against the back of my neck and breathed warmth into me. "Lean into me as if I were a tree," David coached. "Let me be your trunk." I pressed myself into David and felt his ribs smooth over my expanding vertebrae as we formed a breathing, huddled mass. It was the first time we were both physically and emotionally synchronized that weekend. *Give me your tired, your poor, Your huddled masses yearning to breathe free.*

Our bodies may topple into lifelessness while our spirit remains lit.

"This is shit," I repeated. "You have to excuse my language. I know it's not right to swear at a memorial, but this is just shit. For those of you experiencing suicide for the first time, welcome to the LGBTQ experience."

I remembered how minutes after Matt died, my inbox flooded with queries asking if he'd either killed himself or died of an overdose; another young gay man died that weekend from using cocaine laced with fentanyl. From the queer perspective, it seemed unfathomable that dying from injuries sustained in an accident would be a natural cause of sudden death. Many of my gay friends and acquaintances live with the nihilistic assumption of predestined fates: suicide, overdose, disappearance, murder, or AIDS. This is not our destiny, and yet I find myself gay-tired of candlelight vigils.

My gay identity formed and grew around a heightened aware-ness of death; my coming out was set to images of Matthew Shepard. I remembered the friends over the years lost to the fates. I remember the gay bashings and the slurs shouted from car windows. I remembered walking en masse from the village to Victoria Street for a friend who was beaten and run over by an SUV late one night. I remembered how the posters of the missing South Asian men on every streetlamp made me queasy.

I remembered the Toronto police's negligence as they allowed a serial killer to lurk inside the community, how the flower planters of affluent Toronto homed his victims' bodies. I remembered sobbing on the phone to my sister after the shootings at Pulse nightclub. I remembered the memorials, the vigils, the millions killed by AIDS. I remembered the photos of ashes spread on the White House lawn; the bathhouse raids; the memorial for homosexuals persecuted, castrated, and murdered in Nazi concentration camps. I remember Turing, age forty-one, and Lorca, age thirty-eight, and Wilde, age forty-six. To be a gay man is to witness the destruction of the body, from the outside in and the inside out. It is to be branded a survivor until you no longer survive.

"David mattered. I reminded him every chance I had that he mattered."

I welled with anger and my lips tingled.

I wanted to scream "plague" like Larry Kramer. This plague, however, is a scourge of isolation, developmental trauma, fractured intimacy, and shame. It's the panopticon of social media, the surveillance of relationships, and the fragmentation of community. It is the swimming lanes that queers divide their relationships into, a grandfathered pattern of the closet that allows us to fall through the worn fabric of society. It is the plague of capitalism and white supremacy. It is Neo-Victorian America where a marginalized person walks into a hospital in crisis and is turned away because they don't have health insurance.

"I need you to know: in the last days of his life David was held. He was shown love and support and kindness. But the care I offered wasn't enough. I didn't know the whole of his experience," I choked through tears. "I feel like I've failed David and all of you. I'm sorry."

I walked from the microphone stand, feeling clumsy in my emotions.

Cathie once told me that embarrassment is the cousin of shame.

~⋆~

My strap pulls at my shoulder as my black duffel bag clunks against my leg. I run, trying to steady its perpetual motion with my right hand. I'm weighed down, and I don't know if I will close the gap.

"David!" I scream.

David stops and turns to see me running towards him. He smiles and walks in my direction. We meet on the cement promenade underneath the highway overpass. Our lips meet. I smell his cologne. I take his hand before I walk home to Ruby Street.

You killed him.

I stared at the ceiling of the basement apartment a few doors up from Rachael and John's. The next morning had arrived, and my concerns had manifested: there was nothing left to do but feel the entire brunt of this impact. My body was frozen and sunken into a slightly deflated air mattress. I couldn't move, and I had no interest in attempting to rise. A hot iron was pressed against my ribs, and my lips were sandpaper. I didn't constrict the flow of pouring tears that pooled in my eye sockets. I could let my body's entire supply of water spill onto the hardwood floor until the homeowner upstairs barged in to address the flooding issue, only to discover my dehydrated carcass. I knew I should call for help before I became human jerky.

This is a new rock bottom. You have never been this deep before. Get up.

I can't.

Shawn, get up now!

I killed David.

That's not true.

I heard a buzzing sound resonating like teeth chattering against wood. The trance I was under broke. Across the room on a dining table sat my black electric toothbrush. It buzzed and pulsed inconsistently. It vibrated and rattled against the bleached IKEA wood. It emitted different frequencies as it moved between cleaning modes. The toothbrush wasn't connected to any power source. No one else was there. It just flashed (whiten to gum health) and stopped and started (gum health to deep clean) while edging itself towards the edge of the table (deep clean to tongue care) until it fell off and continued its loud rattle on the hardwood floor. Unnerved, I pulled myself from the air mattress and slumped towards the toothbrush. I grabbed my keys, slipped on my sneakers, pulled on David's sweater, and ran out onto Boise Street into a beautiful sunny California morning toothbrush in hand. I took the fifteen or so steps downhill and knocked on Rachael's garage door until Loren answered.

"Hey, are you okay?" She looked worried. "What's going on? We've been texting you."

"Oh, I'm not okay. I'm probably losing my mind, but that doesn't matter because look!" I said, holding up the vibrating toothbrush. "It's David! He's haunting my toothbrush!"

"What!?"

"I was in a really bad place, and for no reason, my toothbrush turned on, and it won't turn off. I was freaked, so I brought it over to you!"

"Holy shit!" Loren's eyes widened. "David is in your toothbrush!"

The members of the grief camp gathered around a table in the basement of Boise watching the toothbrush turn off and on, interjecting itself in our conversation. We were all stricken with a twenty-hour emotional flu. The symptoms included projectile tears, exhaustion, and stiff hearts.

"What's going on down here?" Rachael said, coming down the stairs.

"Not much," Loren replied casually. "David's just communicating to us by haunting Shawn's toothbrush."

"Okay?" Rachael stared at the toothbrush trembling around the coffee table.

"David says, 'Hi Rachael.'" I giggled.

Laughter filled the basement.

It was genuinely crazy to believe that a poltergeist was occupying my Sonicare toothbrush like it was a plot point in *Stranger Things*. A paranormal investigator would conclude the control button stuck, caked with a sticky residue of dried spit and toothpaste. Sometimes we must let ourselves feel haunted to propel us towards the safety of others.

The collective made our way up Bernal to shake off the jitters from multiple pots of espresso and warm milk. We saw a rope swing in a mature tree by the communication tower as we rounded the summit. In all my journeys up and down Bernal, I had never noticed the swing. One by one, we took turns pushing each other, grown adults yelling "higher, go higher" at each other while screaming in terror and joy. "Now, your turn!"

What a gift to celebrate your beloved, then find a swing.

The tragedy was that David didn't get to experience his amassed community's healing power, the moment when the smart, sensitive, and emotionally present people who loved him turned to face one another. When their breaths dropped and they saw each other. One of the longings I shared with David early on was to be in community and not feel isolated in my experience. The difficult task seemed to be locating people who shared my values. If values are expressed as actions, then what do my people do? They celebrate, dance, support, move, deep-dive, drink coffee, share book recommendations, weave, hike, sit, honor, root themselves, make, eat, create, host dinners, foster curiosity, grieve, tie each other's shoelaces, cry, show up, and push each other on swings. Most importantly, my people laugh and make terrible puns. If there was one characteristic that bridged difference and eased us through suicide loss, it was our humor. Collectively we shared the same joyful language of laughter, and it saved many lives — including my own.

Grief camp continued for the rest of the week. There were meditative walks in Tilden Park; strolls along Crissy Field boardwalk; sand dollar collecting along the shores of Fort Funston; happy hour cocktails at El Rio, a gay dive bar, before one last group dinner at Boise Street. Tables pushed together poured past the dining room into the living room. Everyone brought a bottle of wine. Every bottle was opened and placed on the table to be drunk, and Maureen's homemade chocolate babka was the star dish. Tokens of remembrance were exchanged, followed by a moment of silence; glasses were raised and chimed together over and over. It was a celebration of life in every way imaginable while holding space for the one person missing at the table. I sat across the table from Damien. He was the perfect camper to be folded into the grief kibbutz. Damien's energy was light and his humor was sharp. I loved hearing his stories of David. We poured each other wine and passed each other food like it was a practiced weekly ritual. Perhaps it was his broad chest and perfect posture, perhaps it was the wine, but I recognized someone I hadn't felt since October.

In Damien, I felt the presence of Matt.

Hi Bert.

Elby?

Let it be messy.

The first suggested image is to "float."

We begin by waking the body with gentle fluid movements: shifting weight side to side, massaging the moons of our feet into the sprung floor, kissing our shoulder blades together. My hands hang like eggplants and ripen on the vines of my arms. My wrists roll smoothly with the tension of a baby's fist. The sensation of floating comes from the littlest engagement with the musculature of the body. Floating is the effortlessness in staying upright and challenging gravity. Floating is the cooling sensation on the skin from a current of air generated by humans moving in space together. Floating is a defiant statement that says we do not allow ourselves to be shaped by gravity.

We are submerged like reeds in gentle whirlpools of our creation, and the studio is a stream. I float, holding space for others. We face each other in a circle. We move with our eyes open. The work is to hold multiple experiences, both the internal and the external. As I scan my body for tension, I notice the tightness of others. When I ask myself, *Where am I blocked?* I also ask for the dancer across the room. When I breathe movement into that constriction, I create not only room for myself but room for others.

The freedom of my movement is dependent on the freedom of others.

The morning light shines through the stained-glass windows of the studio, and the mirrored walls are hidden with theater blacks. Each Sunday, we gather to have a deeply human experience and to awaken our bodies. Dance is now my weekly soulful practice, and I have found a community of movers who are doing the challenging work of being present with each other and returning to aliveness.

During class we research our bodies and learn Gaga, the movement language of the Batsheva Dance Company of Israel. The class is ninety minutes of constant movement using prompts of vivid imagery and a glossary of euphemisms for the elementary ideas found across movement practices, from dance to yoga to pilates. Tapping, slapping, stretching, shaking, quaking, and flexing ourselves with varying intensities, we find nuance and texture while mapping old, repetitive movement patterns to discover new expressions. Gaga is a sweaty process of transforming pain into pleasure by allowing your bones to expand, your flesh to stretch, and indulging in the moments when you give yourself goosebumps.

The result is an intense sensation of euphoria and ecstasy pulsing through the body, a self-generative state reminding you that aliveness, that sense of wow, is accessible from within.

The researchers are of all ages and body types. Some are professional dancers, some are former dancers, but many enter with no background in dance. Part of my practice is to notice movements based in ambition, both my own and others', and mentally label it "performing." I admire the dancers, but I learn more by practicing with the senior citizens or the stiff office workers as they carve new grooves and reconnect to forgotten sensations. I'm curious about the geyser of information they receive as they slowly explore the extension or "the rope" of their arms. It's all data. The room is a collection of bodied experiences, and I imagine I am a telephone switchboard. I am merely plugging myself into various jacks and eavesdropping on millions of synapses.

I arrived at Toronto's Gaga community wearing one of David's black "The Future Is Feeling" T-shirts. I came to class in memory of David, but I showed up for myself. After the memorial, I felt the language center of my brain collapsing; I felt failed by English. The rapid deterioration of my speech was a warning sign and if I had had permission to scream through a yoga practice, that would have helped — but only in part. The feeling of being speechless is not a fuzzy loss of words, but one of asphyxiation, of panic, of being buried alive. I did not want to surrender to gravity. I knew Gaga was a foundational block of David's methodology, a practice that helped him regulate his nervous system. Gaga was a gift of language to express my sorrow, a road map back to the living, the Rosetta Stone to David-speak. When I dance, I continue to sit in complex conversations with my lover.

I feel not only David, but also invite Matt in the room.

Every class, I use this powerful movement language to begin mending and stitching time in my body. I learn not to collapse into sensation or turtle my back. When my brain wants to punish my body, the body blossoms in an alternate response. When my brain transports me to the subway station, my body takes the hand of David. When my brain passes by Matt's bathroom, my body blows out the candle. I give myself permission to experience the comfort of altering a fated action. It transforms a memory of pain into pleasure. When my chest quakes, I shake my body with intensity in chorus with the flutter above my heart, not against it. When I feel numb, I lovingly slap my skin from head to toe and feel the sting resolve to a tickle. With each flashback, the overwhelm becomes less and less, but how long I will remain a pathfinder is unknown. I accept that managing my flashbacks and chronic grief may be a lifelong healing practice. But skilled with a somatic language, my grief becomes an opportunity to express gratitude for the body I inhabit and for the moments of joy I share with others.

Dance is a discussion between permanence and impermanence, and by moving my body, I am in conversation with my mortality. I feel my skin and muscle move over my bones, and I know that my flesh is temporary. I am two hundred and six dense bones wearing a suit of tissue that is alive. When I stretch, kick, spin, jump, I am reaching for the edges of my human experience. When I am dancing, I feel the burning sensation in the muscles, the release into pleasure, the cooling sweat from open pores, but I am listening to my bones. When my toes, neck, pelvis, or jaw cracks, I am reminded that I am an animated skeleton. Moving the body becomes an act of defiance against gravity and the inevitable. I am not shaped by gravity: I move in connection with the force but I do not give up.

To dance is to laugh in the face of death, and my movement is an act of reverence for my loves who are now a rubble of bones and ash.

November 2, 2019

"When was the last time you sat in a park on a Saturday night?"
I asked the gang.

We relaxed on a lush grass embankment, watching the crowds
gather in Potrero del Sol, a curvaceous green park tucked in the
west end of the Mission district. The late afternoon sun burned
bright with unseasonably warm fall weather. The scraping of
skateboards on the nearby bowl ripped into the silent moments
between tuning mariachi bands, pan flutes and drums warming
up, and plosive microphone check-check-one-two-threes on a PA
system. I looked over towards Rachael and John with their legs
outstretched and angled towards each other. Damien sat like a
merman wearing what I call "my favorite vest."

The falling sunlight painted them and everyone in the park
with a rich smoothness, and I instinctually wanted to draw a
frame around the moment and preserve it with my iPhone. But

my technology could neither capture the gradient of light nor the feeling of care, belonging, and friendship that had taken root. We settled into local time, the time specific to our place on earth, under the system of stars and moon. The poetry of life stepped to the forefront and everything seemed harmoniously crafted, choreographed, and slower. We watched what happens when people are synchronized in intention and care, within themselves and with each other. In this protracted sense of ease, neither day nor night, we invited our ancestors to come and visit. An ancient relationship to time was restored as a gentle warm sensation smoothed over my body.

"This feels like a movie, does it not?" I felt full of wonder.

Rachael broke her focus and smiled in my direction. "Yup, it certainly does."

Damien nodded.

My attention turned to Gemma making final adjustments and lighting candles on the ofrendas at the foot of where we were seated. Side-by-side offerings: a table for David styled in traditional fashion, honoring his Mexican heritage, and a thatched antique dining chair for Matt, interpreting and acknowledging the customs of Day of the Dead. David's table was covered with his favorite swatch of linen, tiered with personal effects, colorful handprinted papel picado, handmade orange pom-poms, framed photos, a mug of cold brew, his memorial program, fresh alstroemerias. Matt's chair sat on a pink rug sprinkled with purple dried bougainvillea collected from Rachael's garden. Fresh yellow marigolds and daisies climbed up the legs, a bunting of photos, an owl mug, some chocolate chip cookies, a tiny green statue of Santa Muerte, and other miniatures. On both, we included pinch pots of salt, coffee beans, and water, along with sugar skulls to welcome our loved ones.

As I have come to understand it, Día de los Muertos celebrates a belief that our beloveds do not die, though they change physical form; they become ancestors who remain alive as a part of the social conversation. They are honored each year with an altar on a night when the veil between the realm of the dead and living is considered the thinnest. On this night, many Mesoamerican families visit gravesites to clean and decorate them with flowers and candles; they prepare heavily seasoned foods, baked goods, and a traditional bread called pan de muerto; they offer gifts such as new clothing or toys; they serve strong coffee, rich chocolate, and libation; they tell stories and sing from dusk until dawn — all for their ancestors. The dead cross over, following a trail of marigold petals and candlelight to be with their families in a celebration of music, dance, poetry, and food that weighs both life and death, joy and sadness, humor and reverence.

The traditions and folklore of Day of the Dead became my singular focus following David's memorial. I needed to go beyond the introduction provided by *Coco*. The animated film resonated deeply with David, and he found comfort with each rewatching; we played its theme song "Remember Me" at his memorial, followed by a moment of silence. I found myself at the library reading books on Oaxaca, death rituals, Aztec gods, the Spanish introduction of Catholicism, and satire as a reaction to colonization. My new learning pointed to a lack in my death education; in my family, we abandon our relatives in cemeteries for a bland buffet spread at a nearby community hall. In death, my ancestors become dusty photos in frames on out-of-tune pianos and not spirits woven into our conversations. In my culture, a wide detachment from death makes the mere concept of sitting with, cooking for, or singing to our ancestors seem foolish or uncomfortable. In my culture, creativity is not valued or nurtured but feared and snuffed out as early in childhood as possible.

Creativity as a pathway to healing means recognizing the unity of life and death. When more room is opened for grief and remembrance, we invite play between natural and supernatural, fact and fiction, myth and science, and intuition and rationality. Through the mysticism of the erotic we invite magic back into our lives and we experience moments of aliveness, an enduring force so true and pure it cuts through the deepest of sorrows.

"What incenses are traditionally used in your culture?" asked Lila, the organizer of the Festival of Altars.

"Glade aerosol," I said. "Clean Linen or Lavender Vanilla."

She laughed. "Perhaps stick to copal or palo santo."

The festival offered workshops to meet the organizers, ask questions, participate, and learn the folk arts of face painting, cutting papel picado, and constructing an ofrenda. Rachael and I attended with many questions about our possibly appropriative behavior that included "Is it okay if we burn copal?" We'd done our homework, but rising above cultural tourism meant making connections, meeting the fellow participants, exchanging ideas around grief, sharing photos; it meant grabbing the broom and sweeping up the shards of tissue paper on the studio floor. The call was to engage in a communal experience, not to imitate a gleaned understanding from a textbook.

Rachael and John's generosity was above and beyond: they invited me to stay in their basement, craft in their garage, and dine at their table. The preparation was a full-week scavenger hunt of ducking in and out of the Mission shops with Rachael, buying fresh tortillas, marigolds, mole, and fruit in preparation for a Friday-night dinner party. "Estoy haciendo dos ofrendas para mis amantes," I said in broken Spanish to small business owners who helped me find appropriate icons and figurines; the local thrift shops would provide a bounty for the altars. Gemma and I hauled the makings of a fiesta back to Bernal Heights in time for David's community to arrive. John spent the afternoon making the main dishes. Rachael lined her front staircase with tea light candles and marigolds to welcome guests and any spirits without family to join. As the collective arrived, we sat around the breakfast nook, making paper flowers using the technique shared with us at the workshop, and everyone brought a personal item to add to David's ofrenda. We drank wine and feasted on tamales, enchiladas, guacamole, jícima and cucumber salad, and Maureen's chocolate chili cake. We shared memories of our beloveds around the table, and I told the folklore of Matt, whose photo joined David's in the living room. I introduced Matt to Rachael, John, and Gemma, to Damien, to all of David's community. We had our moments of silence, of reflection, of community sprinkled between joyous laughter.

An hour before sunset the ritual began in the park, and a large crowd gathered around the five community altars. Four of the altars represented an element (Air, Water, Earth, and Fire) and marked a cardinal direction; they encircled the fifth altar, a giant spiral maze of orange marigolds representing Infinity. The pageantry of costumes and drumming began, and one by one each element was called upon and honored through readings and a display of pantomime by players in Indigenous dress. When Water was introduced, the crowd's attention turned west to a four-post bed fitted with white linen pinned with thousands of plain white tags under a photo canopy of a satellite weather swirl; the 2,975 tags represented the lives lost in Puerto Rico as a result of Hurricane Maria in 2017. Grief is political. It was moving to witness a marginalized Latinx community, targeted by ICE and dog-whistled by a paper towel–throwing president, visualizing ongoing loss. The bed evoked the AIDS quilt, the moccasins of murdered and missing Indigenous women, the white bike memorials of killed cyclists; this arresting expression was where most of the complex conversations of our time need to begin.

My chest tightened as my attention was brought south towards Fire.

"We honor Fire, for Fire brings both life and death. We thank you for all that you provide, Fire. We welcome the spirits, those who have perished from its force to now join us."

Tears formed and my hands found their way to prayer position; my lips kissed the top joint of my thumbs. In the early Aztec tradition, the afterlife was imagined as a path of realms. Everyone was rewarded an afterlife. It was not how you lived, but how you died that determined where you went in the numerous strata of planes. Those sacrificed by fire entered the highest realm of light. *Matt died by fire. He is no longer. He is light.* I expressed my gratitude towards the very force that took him, as fragrant pine copal smoke billowed and candles illuminated the night. This calm and reverence was a juxtaposition to a week where thick acrid smoke wafted over the bay, ghosted the skyline, to where parts of Sonoma still remained engulfed in flames and climate refugees slept in RVs parked on the side streets of San Francisco and Oakland.

I have come to the opposite edge of the continent to confront and befriend Fire. The fire that burned inside my chest, that claimed Matt's life, that caused David to boil over, that rages across the bay.

~ ~ ~

The smoke was faint along the northeast coastal trail that connects Sutro Baths to the Golden Gate Bridge. I was bending time (as David taught me) with a three-hour reflection that started at 5:38 Eastern Time and ended 5:38 Pacific Time. The map provided by the information center at Lands End failed to convey the topography and what looked like a forty-minute hike was two and half hours of trail walking, climbing up and down beaten paths to inlets, and scaling embankments on steps fashioned from logs and chains. I was sweaty, winded by the air quality, but in awe of the crashing waves and cliff formations.

I found myself on Marshall's Beach just minutes before it had been a full circling of the sun since I'd collapsed alone on the floor of an admin office of Sunnybrook Hospital, wailing in sorrow. I dug my feet into the sand and rock as the tide rolled out. Across the Golden Gate Strait were the black volcanic beaches of the Marin Headlands. I measured the distance between that shore and myself, the dangerous currents and frigid waters between, and I felt rooted in the lightness of the white sand and rock on which I stood. I wanted to shed the black mourning clothes I'd been wearing like an Italian nonna for a year. It was the perfect realization to have while on a gay nude beach (second to the realization that I had stumbled onto a gay nude beach). A quick Google confirmed that I was about to observe a sacred moment while naked men popped up like gophers from the man-made rock eagle nests formed along the shoreline.

As this first anniversary of Matt's death had drawn closer, a sense of dread and sadness snowballed. I started to sink in Toronto while mentally planning the occasion, shaping exactly how, what, and where I would/should feel. This pressure was further compounded by people predicting how I should feel on October 29. Having been in a practice of grief, of honoring my emotions for three hundred and sixty five days, I needed someone to bravely say these milestone moments are for the living. I didn't want to predict or perform, but listen to the moment. That meant skipping town, away from the community I shared with Matt to be oceanside and moving my body. A place I could just be.

My alarm sounded: 2:37. I played "Songbird" by Fleetwood Mac softly so that I could still hear the waves.

I looked out to the Pacific, and the sun shined brightly overhead. I missed him beyond comprehension, but it was not a sorrowful moment.

I am alive. I am here by the grace of nature, the support of my community, and the care of professionals. I hold nothing but gratitude.

The song ended.

To my right was a postcard view of the Golden Gate Bridge. A leathery beach rat of a man walked out from behind a rock wearing only a cock ring and stood directly in my view.

"The veil is thin in San Francisco," he shouted to me. "The golden gates are a natural geological threshold."

I burst into laughter.

The park was illuminated with candlelight and the ofrendas that lined the winding pathways came to life. *The spirits have arrived.* Pedestrians walked through plumes of copal, visiting hundreds of ofrendas; they took photos and asked questions about the deceased. Some participated by posting a piece of paper with the names of their ancestors onto a chain-link fence with pegs; others lit candles or painted their faces like skeletons. Recorded history is uncompromising: it concerns itself only with "facts" and not the inner emotional landscape of humans. Día de los Muertos counters that through color, intimacy, and emotion. The vibrancy of the dead come through the whimsy of the details included on the altars and in the storytelling, the personal testimonies, offered by the living. It is an intimate exchange between those who manifest the shape and color of their loss and the bystanders who hold an open curiosity towards it. In this exchange I felt the presence of the dead.

I looked at Matt and David resting side by side, lit by candles and crowned with a horseshoe of moonlit cypress trees above; strangers leaned over to inspect the fine details, and children sprinkled crushed marigolds at the base of the altars. This was the shape of my love and loss.

I scattered a few remaining bougainvillea flowers on Matt's altar, and a woman knelt beside me, flanked by her madre and abuela.

"Did you construct this?" asked the woman.

"Sí, Matthew era mi ex-esposo y David era mi amante," I answered, pointing to my left and my right. "They both passed this año . . . con cinco meses aparte."

The three women were on vacation from Mexico, and an intergenerational, cross-cultural conversation in two languages began. Questions about how Matt and David passed, their careers, what they were like were passed down in Spanish from Madre and translated into English by Nieta, answered in English by me, and translated back up into Spanish. Abuela mostly nodded throughout the conversation before finally speaking.

"¿Por qué pusiste a Matthew en la silla y no en la mesa?" asked Abuela.

"My grandma wants to know why you chose the chair for Matthew," Nieta translated.

I considered my answer because it hadn't been a conscious choice, just an emotional image. "Because there is now an empty chair at our Sunday dinner table. It's where his absence is most visible for my family. It's a way for me to express that in life and in death, Matt will always have a seat at my table."

My answer was translated into Spanish to Abuela, and she wept. She spoke in a monologue, and a chain of tears cascaded down from mother to daughter to daughter.

"She says," Nieta condensed as she translated, "basically, she says this is one of the most beautiful and respectful representations she has ever seen. It shows your love and care . . . and that you should be proud of how you honor her culture and your love."

"Gracias, Abuela." I looked to her.

And then three tearful women hugged a grieving stranger in a park, and they bid me buenos noches.

Rachael and I were left to tend to the ofrendas as a chill grew in the air and the others moved on with their evenings. I watched her introducing herself as David's "City Mom," and I admired how she claimed a title and represented her son to strangers. She had grown a bit agitated by the cold and by the befuddled reactions that someone as young and attractive as David would complete suicide.

David was (and continued to be) failed by the symmetry of his face and physique; his exterior didn't reflect his suffering. Most of us go through life without the privilege of symmetry, and we assume beauty equals a free pass. David would often confess that people didn't see him. I didn't know David as the artist kid growing up in Florida or the demigod performer who danced on the Acropolis, or the marketing whiz who rose in the ranks of ad agencies. I didn't have stories of us dancing sweaty in a Brooklyn bar, attending a friend's wedding, or floating in the Dead Sea. That was not how I was to know him. I knew David as a cartographer who mapped his nervous system, who developed a methodology to regulate the big sensations he experienced in his body. I knew him as someone who challenged me to be present, who saw beyond a disembodying developmental trauma, and who often pushed me to the edges of my love. I saw David, and I held him when he was his most jagged and uneven. Still, I can attest that he was a beautiful, asymmetrical, complicated, funny, and loveable human worthy of care and compassion. He mattered inside and out.

Our relationship was brief and intense, and I don't know what it means to meet and fall in love with someone in the last year of their life. I'm not a philosopher. But you're never on the same path as someone. Sometimes paths run parallel, sometimes they weave in and out, sometimes — unfairly — one path ends before another.

By nine o'clock, Rachael and I had grown tired. LARPers in Medieval dress began tooting madrigals throughout the park, and the plot was beginning to stray. "You know the baseline for what is normal is much broader in San Francisco," Rachael advised on the anything-goes city. As the energy shifted in the park and the cold (for California) settled in, we could envision

Netflix and wine in our future, and I saw a full night of sleep in the comfort of Rachael and John's basement. We were breaking down our offerings when a soccer-ish mom and her preteen son stopped in front of David's table. The tween looked closely at the photos of David as Rachael and I introduced ourselves to the mom.

"This doesn't make sense. He was young and handsome." The curious tween didn't break his focus on the photos. "How did he die?" the boy asked, looking up at me.

"Well." I paused, glancing at Rachael, before giving an oh-shit look to his mom. "With your mom's permission, I will tell you how he passed."

"Please tell my son how he died."

I took a breath. "David was really sad. He was in a lot of emotional pain, and he believed that he no longer wanted to live. And so, he acted on his thoughts, and he ended his life."

"We'll talk about it when we get home," the mom explained, her eyes wet with tears. "Thank you for telling my son, and I'm sorry for your losses."

I couldn't think of a more important conversation to have with a boy on the precipice of extreme emotional and physical change, growing up in the age of persuasive technology.

Death is a conversation for clear nights and still winds.

The next evening I climbed Bernal Hill to take in one last sunset, what I knew would be my last California sunset for some time. Something had shifted after I declared a truce with MacArthur Station, Lake Merritt, and Sears Fine Food and with the shadows that no longer cling to me. San Francisco wasn't my home, but it was the birthplace of my soulful awakening. The bay is a place of constant mediation: fog is neither water nor air; coyote neither killer nor pacifist, nature neither developed nor preserved. The incantation of California faded as I unknit David from a future that was no longer. But the city was a persistent lover, and the elements went out of their way to lure me back with a stunning red sunset, as if to reignite an old flame with a poetic promise.

The entire city was in love today. In Precita Park, couples of every identity combination caressed each other, groups of friends gathered for picnics crowned with freshly baked cakes plated on glass stands, dogs retrieved whatever object their doting owners threw between the islands of humans. I sat on the pink rug from Matt's ofrenda, pretending to read the *New Yorker* while drinking Philz coffee and just being. Rebuilding trust with your life happens by noticing the brief moments of being, finding simple beauty while holding faith that any catastrophe is at bay. It is a vulnerable practice of allowing yourself to fall back in love with life, which is much easier to do when you are surrounded by unabashed expressions of affection. Passion flowed between lovers, even on the rugged rock slopes and the bald, rust-colored plateau of Bernal. I found myself alone but at peace amongst the sweater-on-sweater couples performing their red-heart-emoji love for Instagram.

I could feel myself falling back in love with life again.

If death comes in threes, the third and final was my own. It was the final goodbye to the parts and surfaces of me that were annihilated, the pulverized spaces my loves attached to and occupied that were no longer. What looked like devastation from afar felt like intimate and microscopic growth. It was the rock lichen rooting in my exposed bones, the rerouting of sap through healthy flesh, the sprouts shooting up from relaxed pores. It was more than regenerative; it was metamorphosis. The dissonance between inner and outer had made me feel like I was temporarily occupying myself (doing, saying, living experiences Shawn used to enjoy) until I could shed my former self for a larger container. It was unsightly and uncomfortable to be this raw, and even more unsightly and uncomfortable for others to behold. But let them point, let them laugh, let them shy away: this is what it looks likes when the heart stays open, when the unbroken flood of light refuses to be snuffed.

Since we started working together, Cathie has suggested that I draw or paint or sculpt a representation of myself. It's an exercise that paralyzes me. I've only ever been able to describe what I'd do. My fear of being too exacting, or too literal, or too indulgent has prevented me from picking up a pencil, brush, or tool. In one session, I described a highly detailed cage, and then a few months later, I described a giant swath of peacock blue with two round googly eyes. If I were to paint something now, it would be that sunset. California, with its multitudes, was a physical representation of my emotional landscape. I was the sun surging as it touched Twin Peaks, the light that filled the basin and refracted off the mirrored skyscrapers.

An explosion of vermillion rays transforms the hillside to Mars-like terrain, melts my body, and elongates my shadow like an alien. My skin is warm salmon, my flesh gooey caramel, my bones fibrous pulp. My ribs a trellis for vines. My wrists receivers of information. My heart is filled with July fireflies.

I float.

I am overwhelmed by tears.

I am in love.

What a blessing to be alive, to have loved without fear of losing. To have lost and to be given the sensation of falling again.

Matt wraps his fist tight around my index finger.

Feel it.

David places his hand on my lower back.

Feel.

BEGINNING AGAIN

Swaddle me in wool blankets and rest my body on a nest of birchbark.

Instead of pulverizing my bones and pickling my flesh,

lay me in the earth in a jovial pose, sculpt a laughing skeleton for eternity.

Weave a lush pall of orchids, dahlias, marigolds, and bougainvillea.

Place a coin under my tongue for fare; rest lavender on my eyes.

Offer me food for passage: canopic jars full of

coffee beans, chocolate, cinnamon, California citrus.

At my side, place a treasure chest containing the ashes of my loves.

With the scraps of my clothing, sew a colorful bunting.

String prayer flags made from the pages of my unfinished manuscripts.

Bless my belongings into talismans with palo santo and copal,

"May this object anchor you in the approaching storm."

Prepare bowls of gulal, a powdered spectrum of turquoise, magenta, peach.

Pork carnitas, carrot cake, asparagus with salted butter, and pineapple chicken.

Set a place for my spirit, a thatched chair, to join the feast of abbondanza,

mark Air, Water, Earth, and Fire with lit altars so that I may find my way to you.

Scour the city streets for an abandoned Christmas tree,

made golden from neglect; strip it of its branches.

Replant it in the earth and call it north.

Make a maypole of its dry trunk; it is sacred.

Please speak to the fullness of me. Say the words you can no longer hold.

Recite poems, testify to the times I was difficult, impossible.

Express my multitudes, and dare not forget or redact that

I was a lover and the body you mourn brought pleasure to men.

Cover what was me in lyme and earth.

Call forth a Montreal dancer, paint "Eros" across the blades of his back.

Let him dance in meditation round the pole,

invite desire and longing into your grief. Begin to float.

Reveal a klezmer band, a DJ, and a diva, then commence the bacchanal.

From dusk till dawn, dance around a pyre of my furniture,

like witches' chants, lyrics are spells, syncopation is the *both-and–ing* of heartbeats.

Feel your flesh replenish with blood as time stretches further into the night.

Drink strong coffee and sweet bourbon, dry wine and champagne.

Tell ghost stories and awful puns, dress in costumes from my wardrobe.

Laugh and wail from the bowl of your pelvis.

Swing from the trees and throw plumes of color into a zephyr.

Applaud the daybreak, then leave. Return only to remember

the magic night you danced on my grave and made a skeleton.

When Eros smiled at you, and when through tears you asked

for my mother's sweet 'n' sour chicken recipe.

This is my gift for you, a celebration to awaken the senses.

Let my escape be the creative seed that sows aliveness.

Let that burning in your wrist and chest propel you forward

from a winter of sorrow towards the laughter of a vibrant spring.

Let go. Don't look back. Do not dwell. I am behind you.

IN GRATITUDE

I am grateful for Crissy Calhoun, my beloved editor, spell checker of obituaries, and companion in discomfort. Crissy understood writing would be an integral part of my healing (long before I did). She courageously handed me a metaphorical yellow legal pad and assured me there was space for this story in the world. Her trust and sense of care towards Matt and David was long established before we began writing this book together. Thank you for your brave heart, watchful eye, and gentle steering. Catherine Gauthier, my dance partner in death, challenger of ways, and supplier of tissues. Thank you for helping me be present and responsive in my relationships. Loren Davidson, glimmer spotter, soup maker, and codeword generator. Your friendship is the definition of grace.

I am grateful for the kindness, laughter, and memories I share with Amanda Hines, Tiffany Martinez, Daccia Bloomfield, and

Louisa Varalta Bloomfield; the healing collective of Rachael, Damien, Mustafa, Maureen, Teresa, Aaron, Geoffrey, Brian, John, Gemma, Carla, and Julie; the courage of Jonathan Soja, Chris Lorway, Jen Franchuk, Sharron Matthews, Michael Milkanin, Geoffrey Little, Patricia Tuff, Mim Adams, Mary Keenan, and Monika Smith; the understanding of Teresa, Rita, and Greta; the wisdom of Tommy Smythe, Ed Grady, David Hallman, and Rev. Christine Smaller; the teachings of Alvin Collantes, Erick Stewart, and Nancy Silverman; the compassionate care and kind staff of the Ross Tilley Burn Centre at Sunnybrook Hospital; the careful eye of Jen Knoch, and the ECW crew.

I am grateful for the lives of Stefanie Sherk, my stunning and hilarious friend who made it from Niagara on the Lake to Hollywood and the Oscars red carpet; Hal Goldberg, my first American boyfriend (Washington Square is just not the same).

I am grateful for the companionship of Stevie. My heart belongs to cat.

NOTE ON RESEARCH, NARRATIVE, AND METHODOLOGY

Grief manifested an unexpected and voracious appetite for information, and I attempted to consume all of recorded history. I gained clarity with every gleaned fact or connected idea, but then I sat with the challenge of integrating these new learnings into a narrative without clunky citations and stiff introductory phrases. It was an artistic decision not to quote directly from sources, but I must recognize a few key originators who informed the writing of this book.

Pleasure in the absence of fear (especially concerning contraception), my understanding of aliveness, and the erotic theory are guided by Esther Perel's teachings. Readings that further shaped my understanding of the erotic include "Uses of the Erotic" by Audre Lorde and *In Search of Duende* by Federico García Lorca. *Digging the Days of the Dead: A Reading of Mexico's Días de Muertos* by Juanita Garciagodoy offers a comprehensive history and fascinating cultural insights on the Day of the Dead. The effects of the telegraph (in terms of automation and disruption of time) were learned from an engaging journal article called "The Nervous System of Britain: Space, Time and the Electric Telegraph in the Victorian Age" by Iwan Rhys Morus. The "promise of spring" is a tenet of Caroline Myss, who includes the phrase in her many writings, lectures, and interviews. I learned the sobering facts of impulsive suicides in the 2019 *New York Times* article "The Empty Promise of Suicide Prevention" by Dr. Amy Barnhorst; she cites the 2001 medical journal article "Characteristics of Impulsive Suicide Attempts and Attempters" by O.R. Simon in her piece. Further works I consulted: *The Velvet Rage* by Alan Downs, *Mythology* by Edith Hamilton, and *Metamorphoses* by Ovid.

To write this memoir, I created an embodied approach to storytelling — a methodology to safely write about traumatic experiences while encouraging artistic vulnerability. *The Body Keeps the Score* by Bessel van der Kolk, Ohad Naharin's Gaga (the movement language of the Batsheva Dance Company), and *A Christmas Carol* by Charles Dickens were foundational in this development. My process would not be viable without creative hygiene. The oeuvre of Dr. Clarissa Pinkola Estés was vital to this, specifically her audio works *Theatre of the Imagination*, volumes I and II, and *The Creative Fire*. Finally, it feels essential to state that I was under the care and guidance of a licensed therapist during the creation of this work.

This book was largely written and edited during the great pandemic that began in 2020 — a time of significant loss, much uncertainty, fear, and collective grief, but not without surprising moments of joy, laughter, and clarity.